Tilting Toward the Moon

LitGarden Writers Anthology II

Tilting Toward the Moon

LitGarden Writers
Anthology II

Buffalo, New York

ISBN 979-8-218-13883-7

Copies of this publication may be purchased online, at local book signing events, or by contacting George Grace at: LitGarden Writers, ggraceart@gmail.com

Front cover design by Donna Grace, photo,
  Moon in Tree

Back cover design by Donna Grace, photo,
  October Night

Layout/Design by Kate Willoughby

Edited by Joe Todaro and Kate Willoughby

Table of Contents

Introduction

What follows in these pages is a recent litany of our responses to events, both internal and external, of the past few years, some noted here against our will: love and death, sickness, a lingering pandemic, the Capitol insurrection, war in Europe, continuing racial and gender injustice, and a dearth of political and moral accountability, along with humankind's seeming predilection for self-destruction.

We are students, teachers, artists, activists, travelers, judges, sisters, musicians, historians, gardeners, and mathematicians, unified, not by sameness of style, but by our substance and practice of providing support and inspiration to each other.

This collection of work, varied in theme and scope, may be best approached as the defiant insistence that we must keep trying to make sense of it all, holding close our values, our hope, and all that which we love, whatever the circumstances. Like gardeners - realists, yet optimists - we plant, tend, and reap, and look for some light to grow – even in adversity, as well as in joy - from the bedrock of who we are.

Please read on, as we are *Tilting Toward the Moon.*

Joe and Kate

"If war has an opposite,
gardens might sometimes be it…"
- Rebecca Solnit, *Orwell's Roses,* 2021

"Still, it might not be a bad idea, every time you commit an antisocial act, to make a note of it in your diary, and then, at the appropriate season, push an acorn into the ground."
- George Orwell, *A Good Word for the Vicar of Bray,* 1946

"Our job is to make life worth living on this earth, which is the only earth we have."
- George Orwell, *Reflections on Gandhi,* 1949

List of Art Works and Photographs

Daniel Haskin

Daniel Haskin is the author of seven books of poetry, featuring *Rain Flowers* (2020), and his newest book, *Scripted Life* (2022). He lives in Buffalo, NY, and is a

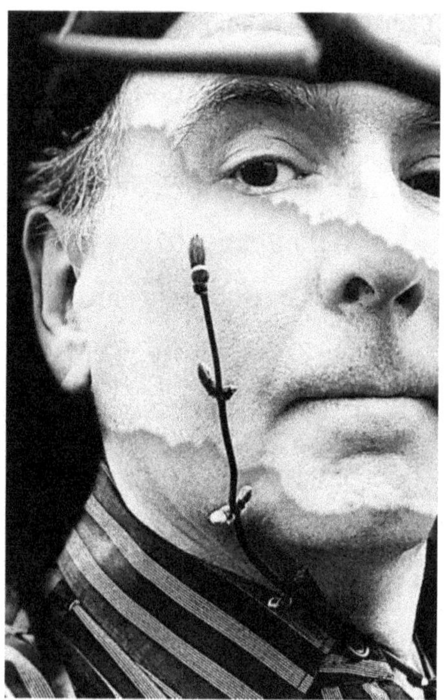

member of the LitGarden Writer's Group. His poems have appeared in *The Buffalo News, Snapdragon Journal of Art and Healing, The Ekphrastic Review*, and elsewhere. He has released two albums of electronic music, and his compositions have been presented on BBC Radio.

Daniel is also a member of the Buffalo Society of Artists, and is a past juror of the Allentown Art Festival. He performed at the Canisius College "Poetry and Music" event (2021). He is currently collaborating with soprano Tiffany du Mouchelle on their neoclassical project, "Sitara".

Two Clouds of Different Names

When we lay
in the grass,
speechless and
full of ourselves,
we will follow
the clouds along
as if they are
made of paper,
written into life
in our own
cursive hand
splendor.

Then I will look at you
and call you into me,
until the end of our
timelessness falls,
and you will
come through
to cover me
with your rain
'til there are
no storms
to look
for us,
as we
flow
by.

Swarming

tell me why
the sun is full of moons

this place where we dream
swooning and felined

no dogs here tonight
just bird shadows

swarming

waiting
for wishbones

Bird Born Blue

I turned
into violet
spilling roses
into your mouth
to bring you back
to me, like everything
you are, light and true.

The bend of your heart
became rooted in sky
in what we call love.
Forever is all things
you are, the flower
who lived in sun,
bird born blue,
and you the
poet's wife
so happy
to begin
again
with
me.

Wearing our
mad hats,
our love
fitting,
once
and
all.

Curious of Our Own Creation

Jeanne's song
is curious
of the colors
of the morning,
and the stretch
across the evening
when time
does not exist.

I will follow you
through the grass
and the rain,
where lilies sing
and dazzle, birds
call out beneath
your green unlocked
words,

until we are the air,
the light of winter
above, the saffron sun
glancing down,
singing of yellow,
sunlight is love.

All that ends
does end in love,
in the beautiful
world of home,
where we will
always be,
curious of our own
creation.

Walking Beneath the Sun with My Brother's Hand

The sky is warm as a yellow song
climbing down over our heads.
It's a beautiful world we have fallen from.

Up sea and downwards
my heart opens up into the weightless
rain-slide of your voice,
like dogwood stars igniting from a sunbeam,
I fall into its light.

I will see you tomorrow.
I find you outside, the familiar places
once held tight with our arms.

The drag of your wooden cane,
with the dragon's head
now propped up against my wall,
and the sound of your leather boots
on the train platform
shuffling past the barrier
from here to there, no plans to wait,
your head tilted to the Morning Star,
and you are gone.

The sun, I am told,
will be waving you on
filling my pockets with rain.

In February, We Walk

These restless things sing for winter shadow
stalking hounds hungry for snow

punching the ground like a footnote
a poem of dogs that owns everything

up to their eyes and ears in winter
where the snow pulls like a forest curtain

sinking its teeth into the breathless ground
as harried as paws cracking and kicking

the last corpse of leaf dog-eared green
beneath banks scurrying to meet their teeth

the art of dogs is just a scratch above
the wide clouds that dance

that run beneath the dog star in drifts
up to nose and tail thigh bone deep

beneath the snow-moon
light and glassy as ice cream

the clouds are just
the dogs passing by

Rumble Bells

Hear
the children play
for those who have
died young,

ringing their
rumble bells
over the
hissing dirt,
miming the dead.

I am walking
through them
like a ghost
through rain,

the smell,
cradles' grief,
covering my eyes
like a sixpence.

The sky sings
gray and violet.
the siren is slow
and forgotten.

Propeller Flowers

In my dream
milk is like ink but calm,
like a sea of clotheslines,
a place of drying quietly.
I trip across the sheets,
hung from blue and ladders.

Tilted towards the moon
I climb out midway
from everywhere.

The moon is steep and slow,
from this place
there are no parachutes,
only propeller flowers grow.

Royal Quiet Deluxe

for Anne Sexton

I've been walking the halls
with a stranger's foot,
like a tin ghost,
plotting my steps.
And here you sit,
royal and quiet,
tied with a ribbon,
praying for wrists
and fingertips.
I named you
book and bell,
with keys of snow
and stillborn crows,
poking pinpoints
starry enough
to renovate
the dead.

Poetry is ecstasy
here, a candy moth
into the pitch, the sun,
the star that warms,
the words that dance
on pages of milky paper
hung from half blind trees,
waving, buckling to breathe.
I hunt and peck for words to say,
the bell clangs like a bullet,
but the keys will not stop singing.

An Impression of Noon

In the sky
all birds are open wide.
Their ravenous wings
swell into the air, spiriting.
Bones all filled with floating
as they slide across
the impression of noon.

They taste the sun's bitter flow
that kisses Moon and stars,
all pricked with dots of light,
and no care of somewhere.
Wandering this way, that way,
the hungry clouds
will eat their fill.

Donna Grace

Donna Grace produced a few poems while working as a substitute teacher in the Buffalo Public Schools as she co-hosted the LitGarden Writers Group since 2008. In 2020, at the onset of the pandemic, she quit teaching and took refuge in writing poetry. Her earliest efforts were rewarded with a poem published in *The Buffalo News'* Poetry Page, and she has been a featured reader at the Screening Room, The Dalai Java in Canandaigua, The Buffalo Corner, and "Music and Poetry – A Musical Feast" event at the Montante Cultural Center.

Dreams and Distractions

Time was, a map was a thing to be done with
after the trip,
a crumpled chart of memories
in food stains, coffee rings,
inked-in routes, circled landmarks,
off the beaten paths,
telephone numbers, random notes,
and a confusion of creases
that served as the official record
of every failed attempt at refolding.

I look up from my map-reading
to watch the cat, on a reconnaissance mission
behind the gossamer curtain,
eyeing the trio of blue candles
next to the window,
where prisms from the blue crystal sun catcher
dance on the wall.

The car sits in the driveway,
our suitcases gather dust in the closet,
and next to the atlas,
the tall spines of travel guides and
crossword puzzle books
lean against the wall
in their starched uniforms
waiting for the service bell.

Hope in a Suitcase

After shivering in the car
under the moon and starlit Mojave Desert,
The Weight playing on the radio,
I pulled up to a California ghost town's diner
for scrambled eggs and rye toast,

joining the locals at the counter
sitting on cracked red vinyl stools,
memories swirling
with cigarette smoke and the latest gossip
in the breeze of café ceiling fans.

I stepped into the shade
of the abandoned movie house marquee
that read *Town Without Pity,*
for a brief escape from the heat of the sun
that parched my skin
through blue jeans and a black turtleneck,

I carry the image of my father
that morning I said goodbye—
yesterday, last week, or years ago—
when I watched from the doorway
as he sat in the kitchen in a house not his own,

his calloused hands, workman's arms
forged by long labor in the Open Hearth,
smoothing his thin white hair with nicotine fingers
as if to calm the sorrow pulling down his sunken cheeks,
his round blue eyes speaking their familiar language,
staring off at the ticking red clock on the wall.

Girlhood

In the crackling night air,
selling Christmas Seals for school,
my toes ached from frostnip
as the snow crept into the holes
of my rubber overshoes.

At the sight of the boy in the white jacket,
flanked by his gang like wings on a raptor,
rounding the corner onto the deserted street,
I raced inside an apartment building
and ran up the stairs.

Miss Haley in 2B answered my flurry of knocks,
invited me in to call home.
Mary answered the phone.
We're not a taxi service, was all she said,
and slammed the phone in my ear.
Miss Haley called the police.
We're not a taxi service, was all they said.

Hiding in the darkened hallway,
I counted the beats,
measured the rhythm
of the boys' shadows
as they eclipsed the band of light
cast on the wall from the streetlamp.

I bolted

through the A&P parking lot
to the busy highway,
darted between cars, hopped over snow banks,
cut across back yards,

dodged between buildings.
Home. I locked the door behind me.

In the lamp-lit living room,
my family read newspapers.
The Lion Sleeps Tonight played on the radio.

Only the dishes I washed hours before,
no longer dripping in their rack,
welcomed my return.

Sitting on the bottom cellar stair,
shaking, gasping for air,
lungs on fire,
I glanced at the window.

The boy stared back at me.

A Perfect Day for Wondering

First day of school for my siblings.
But for the sound of mother's
footsteps and the mop
sloshing over the kitchen floor,
the house is quiet.

In the distance a fog horn reverberates,
guiding ore freighters
into the canal.

I scramble eggs in an iron skillet
before heading to the
smooth wooden rocking chair
Uncle Fred made nine years before
in his basement workshop
for my brother, the first born.

By the time it got to be mine,
only a few traces of red paint
clung to the wood grain, chipped and fading,
and the grinning teddy bear sat
in yellow overalls with orange buttons.

The seat, an obtuse angle to lean back on,
the oblong sides with oval thumbholes
to grip, as some children might—
the ones who care about balance and gravity,
a marvel in simplicity.

No one ever tipped backwards
though we dumped forward often enough,
squirming with laughter.

With teddy in my arms,
faded to beige, nose missing,
down one eye, as if to wink,
five years and three sisters old by then,
cotton stuffing bursting at the seams,
we rocked, the two of us,
taking it all in.

Home

While house wrens
settle in bungalows
rocking gently in the breeze
to the lullaby of leaves,

a raven
circles the clouds,
jubilant, as if a warden signed his release
and sent him into the world
with all he needed,

unlike the man just outside the prison gate
set adrift in low-risk blues.

The past of bars and walls
melts into sun-drenched fields,
while he carries his world in a small mesh bag
on his journey into the gloom
that vanishes
as he passes through.

Nightdreaming

I often stood alone in the shadow of Eads Bridge
watching the Mississippi
shimmering in tangerine lights,
winking at me with onyx eyes
carrying the weight of its sordid past
of heartbreaks and delusions
before drifting off,
an outcast, to the open sea.

After sunset,
after the heavy heat settled like a blanket
on the bed of sleepy streets,
I walked along Laclede's Landing.
Crumbling cafes served paltry promises
on balmy nights when
Billie Holiday rose from the mist,
wrapped in the white gardenia air,
singing *St. Louis Blues*
to the sounds of cartwheels
and the lyrical canter of horse's hooves
on the cobblestone carriageway.

Bread and Bisous

If you find yourself in Paris
in a room flooded in February sun,
with doors that open onto a small balcony,
you might view a vignette
in front of a boulangerie across the street
of two men greeting each other—
you know, like those scenes in movies:
hugging and cheek kissing
to the music of happy words.

If one is holding a sack too short for a tall baguette,
he tears off a piece and hands it to his friend,
then tears off a piece for himself
to nibble as they talk, hands flying like maestros,
heads thrown back in laughter
as the loaf meets its crusted end.

And that, too, they share equally,
keeping the tradition of affectionate partings.
After the man with the sack empties the crumbs
onto the sidewalk for the pigeons to peck around,
he returns to the bakery, emerges with a warm baguette,
and stands on the sidewalk,
whistling,
waiting.

Penance

On late Sunday afternoons,
beyond the kitchen window,
the sun slashes through blue gray clouds,
glints off icicles like shards of glass.

I pluck this moment from a mélange of moments,
a sepia photograph framed and
hanging above my memory's hearth:
the long walks to mass with my father
after he pulled down double shifts at the steel plant.

I waited by the door as he came into view,
trudging through deep snow,
weighed down by the knapsack filled with work clothes
slung over his shoulder.

If given a choice, I still would have gone along.
I wouldn't leave him to face, alone,
yet another hostile world.
To what did he owe a patriarchy anyway,
that so despised this poor working man, and his daughter?

Arctic winds fought with me over my hat,
pelted my cheeks,
tore at my fingers through flimsy gloves
clawed their way up my sleeves and down my back,
lashed my bare legs, frost nipped and stinging.

I can still picture my father leaning into the forceful gales
holding the crown of his brown fedora with one hand,
the other tucked deep inside his pocket,
his old brown dress coat flapping against his wiry frame
like a wounded bird struggling to fly.

Captured

Kidnapped? I'm not sure
what word would describe
what happens to me,
but I can tell you,
it happens all the time.

They don't kick the doors in
and roll me up in a carpet and carry me out
and then whisper ransom demands
over the telephone at midnight.

Maybe *hijacked* is the better word,
although I'm not sure
about that, either,
since hijack usually involves
airplanes and I don't fly.

Abducted? How else to describe
an ordeal that occurs while sitting in a chair
in a sunlit room, or under a lamp
reading a book

that grabs me by the scruff of the shirt,
pulls me into a saga
where, without luggage or passport,
I am in a foreign land
to mingle with lives lived long ago
where nothing
is lost
in the translation.

Ode to the Water Gatherers

Blues drift from a neighbor's garage
as the garden hose dances,
snaps around my legs in kinks and tangles,
snags on a car tire, catches on a jagged rock.
Like a fairy waving a magic wand,
I quench the shading trees and cottage gardens.

I think of you in the frying pan heat of Sierra Leone,
wrapped in a sarong, slogging for miles
to ladle forty pounds of dirty well water
into a jerrican you carry on your crown
over a thick cloth halo.

I think of you in your black burqa, in Yemen,
shackled waist to ankle with water jugs
that tear at your legs like talons
on the far journey to your village;

I think of you, so far from home,
in monsoon-flooded Myanmar,
your small bare feet slog through toxic mud,
neck bent under buckets of foul water
that pitch and heave off the shoulder yoke.

Two boys bolt from behind me on bicycles,
ride through the spray, legs splayed,
belt out whoops and squeals, turn around and do it again,
cooling me in the mist.

Forgive me as I raise my eyes to the snowball clouds
that seem to deepen their blue canvas
as the monarch drops by her milkweed patch
and I fill the bird bath to brimming.

Lynn Ciesielski

Lynn Ciesielski has taught adults and children with disabilities for over two decades, and retired from the Buffalo Public Schools. Her poetry has appeared in *Helix*, *The Buffalo News, Iodine, Main Street Rag,* and other journals and newspapers. Lynn has published a chapbook, *I Speak in Tongues*, and a full length book, *Two Legs Toward Liverpool*. For many years, Lynn has hosted the monthly poetry and music series, *Circleformance*. She spends her time reading, writing, studying, and enjoying her friends and family.

Poem (after Billy Collins)

26

This poem is a two-a.m. wake-up call,
eyes glued to the computer screen,
a full pot of dark roast reeling it forth.

It's an exhale dissolving into tears
once the caffeine spends itself.

This poem climbs mountains past the tree-line,
where there is nothing to grasp
but memory, pain, and lost connections.
It knows there is a pinnacle, but isn't certain
what it will encounter when it reaches it.

This poem is not a soak in a hot spring,
a bath scented with lavender,
or a goose-down pillow you sink into,
releasing the day's struggle.

It's the longest to-do list you've ever faced,
with each item feeling like a few.

It's not a gentle breeze on the first day of May,
or a rain after two years of desert sun.

It is the blizzard that whips your tender face,
the snow bank that dares you to climb it
on your walk home after a twelve-hour work day.

When you reach the final word, it is not
a trophy, a blue-ribbon or an ovation,
just a nod, and a pair of clenched lips.

Sunday, August 30, Mt. St. Mary Academy

Truth told, last place I wanted to sit
that final August Sunday,
was an unforgiving wooden folding-chair,
Catholic high school fade-in
with a smattering of old folks
shifting left to right as I did
on equally miserable bottoms,
truly no fond summer farewell

but for Susan, second clarinet,
lover of corny concert music
who rivals most in devotion,
willing heart and burnout drive,

who woke at four a.m. one icy day
to ferry me to the airport,
knowing at best she'd scrape ten minutes
before her wheat toast, no-butter breakfast
nibbled between long-distance snatches
of a conference call to regale those online
just as the always did for her spin-me-nuts,
round and round, Buffalo to DC research gig
because her oh-so-special adult child
lived a day away from the home office.

To the left, the right, behind and before us
devotees, lovers of *real music*
as all music once was.

We watched this cardboard cutout,
the holiday-decoration kind,

black-clad to match the players,
but comical, with paper fasteners
leaving limbs stiff, yet unhampered movement
made more precise with conducting baton.

Now brass. Now woodwinds. Tympani.
And without notice, the cynic in me fled.

Flutes rose and fairies danced until,
bit by bit, brass built to a crescendo.
Drops spilled from my eyes
as I wondered if the single mistake I pulled
from the perfection was my Susan,
saying *hello* as she promised she would.

(first appeared in Helix Poetry Magazine, Spring 2016)

Last April's Gift

(for Judy)

A bed of green—lush, lavished
with copious blossoms—
brilliant wishes
drenched with sentiment.

It overspills its urn
like the scope of our friendship
moving beyond the limits of its years,

my connection to that visit
when illness stifled me,
but could not stifle what we share.

Is This What Love Songs Are Made Of?

At Dad's shop picnic, only time I tasted
anything better than Fanta red pop
or cream soda, I gave *him* my number
over a birch beer.

We tasted August, chrome dragonflies,
Chevy's union and fate that brought us there.
His curls, a gold that paled daffodils,
rolled me down hills, spun me round carousels.
For days, his name wrote cursive trails, waltzed
through my mind's dance floor.

Half a moon later, he phoned, just as the trails
stopped at a wall.
I'm pitching tonight. Come watch.

Three suburbs over, ninety minutes by bike,
further than I should go, I arrived
just in time for the final out.
I flew toward him, arms open
and kicked dust until words rose.

Great game!
You just got here, he said, leaning into me.

A year older, he must have had some practice,
so I hid my surprise when his tongue,
like a slice of mango, slid through my lips.
To keep my teeth open, tongue unmoving
was harder than pedaling uphill.
(first appeared in *Buffalo News*, March 2015)

The Night That Wasn't

Gabel's neighborhood dive bar,
with a dance floor where we never danced.
Tammy's dimples and wink got us past
every bouncer without ID.

Miller beer, two bucks a bottle,
didn't taste so bad after two or three,
and by the seventh it was liquid sunshine.

Journey, Bon Jovi, and U2 whirled
on the turntable as we slurred gossip and boy talk.
Wobbling to the bar for last call,
the sticky floor was the only thing
that kept us from falling.

I worked my waitress shift at Jimmy's,
two hours left to kill,
so we lit a fat joint on the Jewish synagogue steps,
napped ninety minutes, lids half-shading
our muddy river eyes.

Mostly regulars, my rap sheet established:
jumbled orders, coffee in laps, sloppy math.
Alexopoulos, the owner, tallied my late minutes.
He worked my tables, jotted orders,
playing tag team with the grill.

He slung me my notebook and apron and I was on.

Order one, souvlaki breakfast, white toast, not pita,
I grabbed the nearest knife to cut toast triangles.
The knife slipped, my fingertip unfolded, hung.
Nearly numb, I watched the carmine spill, brilliant,
pooling on Jimmy's yellowed linoleum.

Customer's complaining, Jimmy barked.
What's taking so long?

He handed me a mop to swipe the blood.

I need stitches, I said.

Get a bus! Here's a buck.
Don't tell them where it happened.
And don't ever show your face in here again.

INFLAMED

Seneca—keepers of the Western Door
  Six Nations
        dwellers of Gowanda—under the
cliffs

    Cattaraugus—rushing, fierce like Seneca
    burning stream
      carves   channels
       careens
through Zoar Valley   spilling cascades a
quarter-mile over splintering, shale slopes

    Forests—
      Chestnut Oak   Red Oak
   Pine

Stomping grounds for the Clawfoot people—tale told
      a century old

    This British bawd, it unravels   fell prey to the
syph   her progeny

punished—hence   with fused extremities
    generations carried the curse

Until—
   ultimately, they made a pact—to squelch the
stream, the gene—mate no more

       FORGIVE ME

   I   digress   diverge
    DISASTERS

       still befall   the splendor

deluges   drownings   deaths
     in this daunting

    Playground???

      STRANGERS ignore the warnings—

Slippery shale   mudslides   drastic drops

    Deh-he-wa-mis grouses—
*They trash our lands—   our mother sya di:tgeh[1] them,
angered*
    *In turn we deliver them from their
gaiwane'aksha[2], their brush defiance
tears searing our cheeks like lightning   that ravages
our methane-infused creek.*

[1]evicts   [2]wickedness

(first appeared in *BlazeVox*, Spring 2022)

How Not to Cry

Swallow clouds whole.
Let them rise to your tear ducts
until the droplets dissipate.
Let them join the cycle, vapor to sky to orchid drink.

Blink the tears inside out.
Lock your lids tight so they can't escape
when the visions drown you:
>   -your daughter's rusty cell adorned with
>   photocopies of the kids
>   she gave away alongside a Christmas card
>   Madonna,
>   -your husband's chemo-eaten pipe cleaner limbs,
>   -the man living on a highway ramp, who leaps in
>   front of your car
>   with an outstretched hand.

Turn your woes to iron spikes.
Drive them into your seat and the floor.
Clench the chair arms so tight
your fingernails slit the fabric.

Set them on the wings of monarchs,
swallowtails, and seagulls.
Let them soar to distant lands
where they can hide among strangers.

Stroll the forest. Replace your whimpers
with buzzing bees,
and surging streams.
Become the rustling leaves.
Turn each tear into a dewdrop
and assign it a blade of grass.

Whisper an incantation that transforms
the salty drops to rice grains,
encapsulating riches instead of sorrows.
Cast them at wedding couples.

Bury yourself in a down comforter.
Reconstruct a flock of geese
to fly you to a land where tears reside
when you feel the rush of wings.

Surround yourself with a gaggle of giggling children.
Let their laughter rinse away life's wounds.

Fill yourself with blessings.
Wedge in so many you crowd out
all inklings of hurt.
Let the tears become a celebrated sun-shower
on a day when heat is a tidal wave.

Breathe. Fill your body with cool air.
Chill the sting that sears you
like the hot pan you once picked up bare-handed.
Convince yourself
that the welt is just a rub-on tattoo,
a twenty-five cent vending machine prize.
Breathe.
Just breathe.

(first appeared in *The Buffalo News* in April 2022)

Victims

The headlights hypnotized her.
Butch halted just soon enough to behold
eyes round and gold as the ring
he had worn for thirty years.
He rushed to check the damage to his pick-up.

He and Susan struggled to move
the doe's body from the road.
Susan tasted blame in the bitter air,
replaying like bile on an empty stomach.

Butch insisted that she caused the damage.
Her nagging made it hard to stay on track.

She countered that he *cheated* like always,

when they argued about who would drive.

Why didn't she stay off the road? He pointed.
She should have been aware of the danger.

Susan prayed to the earth to forgive all men
for the acts of those who strayed.

After they dragged the carcass away,
Susan decided to hide the memory.
She wanted no one to see those eyes staring
at the universe like dying stars.

She searched the trunk for the blanket
they kept for messy jobs:
        their daughter's water when it broke early,

poppies from the garden store,
the regular oil changes in the driveway.

She covered the creature's face and
shuffled toward the truck.
Butch handed her the keys and surrendered for the evening.

Do you still want venison for dinner? he asked.

First Heartache

Riding home in the family station wagon
that cloud-cluttered morn,
Sandy squirmed in my lap, wrapped
in a well-worn towel
reeking of D & L residue and the oil it had cleansed.

She warned that she'd tatter our rule book,
shred our upholstery, and chew from the plates
we set ourselves with Benedict breakfasts,
grilled cheeses, and Sunday stews,
plowing fulsome and fierce through our linens.

But those puppy kisses dispelled bully-battered days
like wind scatters dandelions-gone-seed.

And I could forgive the frequent nips even
when they drew blood, because her coat
was velvet twilight and her tail a child on a swing.

Just a month after she came, Dad bellowed,

Back to the SPCA! No more chances!!
waving his Budweiser toward the yellowing rug.

But they'll gas her,

I squealed, tears gushing, arms restraining her as I sat,
cross-legged on the floor, her yelps battling my sobs.

Mom braced me while Dad pried her from my arms
then jammed her puppy-spirit into a tiny, cobwebbed-crate.

Asleep love? Or should we talk?

And my jaws clamp safe-locked,
securing my secrets,
but my brain quakes and ears rumble.
Even my breath spikes
with acute, jagged memories.

I fold their forms
into origami fish,
plunging them beneath cenote waters,
my own live offering
to the dreadful gods that torment me.

Rumbling, my neat creases unfold.
Fins flail and thrash, heaving the depths
to where I've banished them,
creating a tsunami.

I scream, unable to quell their frenzy.

My lover strokes my hair, cooing
until my cries become a monologue,
fragmented images spoken aloud,
ricocheting sometimes until dawn.

cenote: An underground reservoir of water such as occurs in the limestone of Yucatan, Mexico.

My Body Lies

Naked on this bed of nails,
I lie dormant, a numb host
to this spread of sharp spikes
when a memory makes me cringe.

I lie dormant, a numb host,
then unwitting I shift my weight
when a memory makes me cringe,
and a spike pierces a fleshy hip.

Then, unwittingly, I shift my weight.
My body sinks, settling me
and a spike pierces the other hip,
body becoming a cascade.

My body sinks, settling me,
and I exude a seething heat.
This body becomes a cascade
dispersing in rising steam.

A Meager Substitute

These oven-warm cookies
are the hugs
you won't accept
even on momentous occasions,

for touch is a brutal weapon
that connects your skin
with suffering,

and this offer is my attempt
to connect with you,
like when we rode tandem
while I nursed you at my breast.

Alone in the Andes

In Villa de Leyva, there's a pilgrimage,
and it's required, almost, but
my heart, head and muscles groan
as Sara strides, while I drag
foot after hand after face,
panting, cursing thirty years smoking,
forty pounds of impeding weight,

resting just until she reaches the corner
that takes her beyond sight
then climb a few yards more until
she instills that the ridge I straddle,
a third up, is my safe point, and forced
into a choice made for me, questions
pinball inside my head but I ask only,

How long?

Because waiting is forever without a watch,
so I beg a photo for proof, nod goodbye,
then sit alone, a garden of roofs
unfolding before me, but inside,
empty landscapes where no one holds my hand
or knows my name, and fear,
fiercer than banditos, cougars, and flash floods,
sets in until, quivering,

I face an even greater challenge,
seeking balance in the steepest place I know.

(first appeared in *Weekly Avocet*, July 2017)

Michael Delaney

Michael Delaney is a retired Professor of Mathematics at Erie Community College and a former officer in the faculty union - he also ran ECC's professional development for four years. He has written fiction and poetry for 29 years but has been remarkably unprolific. He has published in the Buffalo News, Art Voice, and three anthologies, Gary Earl Ross' "Buffalo Nights," and Scott Williams' "A Flash of Dark II" and "A Flash of Dark III." He is cofounder, with George Grace, of the LitGarden writers' group, which is now 13 years old. He lives in Hamburg, NY with his wife Judy Stenroos, a retired Buffalo elementary school teacher, and their cat, Leo. He has one son, Ivan.

The Phone Call

"Billy, did you hear? The radio stations are asking
everyone who was in the Elbow Room last Thursday to call
their medical professionals. Big-time virus exposure.
Wasn't that Dad's favorite place?"
Billy and his sister Mary Jo are talking on the phone.
Billy asks, "The Elbow Room, on Center Street?"
"Down the hill from Main Street."
"No, you're thinking of Joe's Place. Like Joe Galante."
"That's it, Billy." Mary Jo says. "I was thinking of Joe's
Place."
"The Elbow Room was that college-kid bar on Center just
up from Main. Across from the movie theater."
"Dad wouldn't have gone in the Elbow Room."
"You're right," says Billy. "He would have had to pay for
his own drinks. Joe's was down the hill from Main. I think
it was on Bank."
"I don't think Joe's is there anymore."
"Wait," Billy says. "I can look it up on my phone." He
does. "Yup, there it is. 38 Bank Street. It says, 'Great bar
food.' I don't recall them having a kitchen in Dad's day.
Just snacks. I went in there with Paul a couple years after
Dad died. I don't know if Joe was still alive. They had
changed the decor to appeal to a younger crowd."
"Most of the old townie places are gone now."
"It also says, 'permanently closed.' I think the photo is a
Google Maps street scene. It looks like an empty lot where
the bar used to be. But they've got a phone number and a
button marked 'call.' They even have one of those online
reservation services. For a place that's permanently closed?
And torn down?"
"I think it burned down. I think I remember that," Mary Jo
says. Then, playfully, "Maybe you should call the number."
"It would be funny if someone answered."

"You could ask for Joe."
"I could ask if Dad's there."
"Haha."
"Hahaha."

Later that evening, Billy does something out of the
ordinary. He opens the bottle of Laphroaig he had owned
for more than a year and pours himself three fingers, neat.
He puts on a Puccini opera. He sits in his favorite fat easy
chair for a long time, listening, sipping, smelling the peat,
meditating. Then he pours himself another three fingers.
Shortly after that he decides it would be a good idea to call
the number at Joe's Place.
The phone rings.
"Joe's Place, where the elite meet to get shitfaced. Beetle
speaking. Joe ain't here."
This is followed by raucous male and female laughter and
commentary. "Beetle, you sound like that old show,
Duffy's Tavern!" "Of course Joe ain't here! Joe's never
here!" Other undecipherable hilarity.
Billy, not having planned what to say and feeling under
extreme pressure, absurdly asks for his own dead father:
"Hi. I'm wondering if Charlie Maloney's there?"
"What, Chuck?" Beetle replies. "I don't know. Let me go
look. I'll be right back." Billy vaguely recalls that his dad
had a friend called Beetle.
Billy hears the receiver being set down on a hard surface
with a clunk. He remembers the red wall phone at the end
of the bar next to the street windows. They would let you
use it if you put a dime in the cigar box. Billy pictures the
receiver sitting on the bar facing into the room. He hears
the jukebox. Songs that were on that box in the early
seventies. Songs he would have punched in when drinking
beer there with his father. Bob Seger's "Fire Down
Below." Free's "Fire and Water." Curtis Mayfield's
"Freddie's Dead."

He hears the bar patrons chatting:
"Okay. Four punch lines. All about the same occupation.
Give me each joke and the occupation. Professional
courtesy. A good start. A Doberman Pinscher. And, they
opened the door and there stood the cow and the pig."
"Hey, George! Won't you get us that special bottle of wine
you've got hidden in the cellar?"
"Listen, Randy, don't tell your date that stuff, you know
there's no cellar and no door on the other side, and you
know I can't do that trick anymore. Darlin', I know you're
a grownup, but please think twice."
"And she said, 'But the box said three to five years!'"
"'You mean you've got a drink in here called Larry?'"
"'Okay. Now where's the old bitch with the bad tooth?'"
"And the bartender says to him 'Superman, you're a mean
son of a bitch when you're loaded.'"
"So, the wife says, 'you know, dear, not every man is as
cheap as you are.'"
Steppenwolf's "Born to be Wild" comes on the jukebox.
Billy hears bar stool feet scraping on the floor and some
customers settling in at the bar near the phone. Then two
men talking.
"George, a pitcher of your best Genny for me and my
friend here."
"Jackie, you're the best."
"There is indeed a balm in Gilead, Vick, and here it is. Let
me pour you a glass."
"Does that mean we're in heaven?"
"I don't know. Maybe. This feels pretty good. It might be
Limbo, though."
"Jackie, how long have we been coming here?"
"I don't know, Vick. I don't even know what time I came
in tonight."
Drinking sounds. "Yup, this is good. Just what I needed.
You ever notice how good that first drink of beer tastes?"
"The first one was an awful long time ago, Vick."

James Brown's "Sex Machine" comes on the jukebox.
"Do you ever hear from your kids, Jackie?"
"Yeah, I guess. Last I knew the boy was in California.
Aerospace industry. Married with kids. A boy, a girl,
another boy, maybe another girl…? God's honest truth,
Vick, I can't tell you how many kids he's got or what kind
or how old they are. I keep seeing him as that skinny 30-
year-old he used to be. Pretty wife. Filipino. Are they still
together? I don't know. I can see his kids, little tykes riding
all over those California hills on their Big Wheels. Are they
still little tykes? Or teenagers? Or all grown up? Careers?
Families? I don't know, man. We don't really keep in touch
much. And I tend to lose track of time. Except in here, of
course. I always know what time it is in here."
Vick says, "Yeah, we all do."
"The girl went to New York years ago to try to be a
writer," Jackie continues. "What happened? I wish I could
tell you. I get a Christmas card from her every year. At
least I think I do. There's never any news in it, just 'Merry
Christmas Dad. Love, Julie.' Is she happy? Is she
successful? Does she have a family? I don't know. We
used to play catch in the backyard in the twilight, just like a
father and son. Ah, well. They've got their own lives, am I
right?"
"You're right." Long silence and sounds of drinking.
"Do you miss them, Jackie?"
"Sometimes I miss them something awful, Vick. We had a
lot of fun together. Especially when they were little."
Johnny Cash's "Folsom Prison Blues" comes on.
Vick says, "I seem to remember having a wife, Jackie. I
wonder whatever happened to her."
Then Jackie yells out, "George! Will you take a look at
what it's doing outside? It's snowing like a sonofabitch!
And it's the middle of April! I swear it's the last days, man.
I think this calls for a round on the house!" A smattering of
chuckles and applause.

From a distance, George calls back, "In your dreams, Jackie. Although I probably ought to go out and pour some salt on the sidewalk. If I could ever get away long enough from serving you…gentlemen. And ladies of course. Sorry, Carol. Just be careful out there when you walk home!"

"We're going home?" Jackie asks, sounding confused.

The Doors' "Roadhouse Blues" comes on.

"It's funny," Vick says. "I have a hard time remembering being anywhere else but here."

"Yeah, Vick, I know exactly what you mean."

"Let me pour you another glass of balm, Jackie."

Beetle comes back and picks up the phone:

"Hey, pal. Sorry I took so long. Nobody has seen Chuck tonight. Matter of fact, we haven't seen him in a couple of days. He's usually a regular. I think he was in here night before last. You a friend or relative or something?"

"Yeah, we're related."

"Well, you might want to check in on him. Last time he was in here, he didn't look so good, and he was coughing something awful. Hope he's okay."

"Right. I will check. Thanks."

Billy hears the phone being replaced on its cradle at the other end. He takes another sip of single malt scotch. He thinks about calling the number back just to see if it's really in service. Then he thinks better of it.

The Party

Annie and Denis are throwing a party in their too-small apartment. They provide the devilled eggs, four-layer Mexican dip with corn chips, lots of Denis's homemade beer and wine, and a big crate of LPs. Guests arrive with food and drink contributions. Dance music plays, and some partiers are dancing awkwardly in the cramped space. Signs tell the guests that tobacco smoking is only on the fire escape, cannabis only indoors.

Annie has been hustling like crazy, setting out food and drinks and greeting guests as they arrive. She notices some of them are dressed in costumes. There is a baseball player, a bat (animal), a lobster, various medical and law enforcement personnel, a few Elvises, and several recent US Presidents. All this seems odd to Annie. She didn't advertise it as a costume party, and it seems like the wrong time of year.

Finally, Annie manages to slip away from her greeter role. She finds a corner where she can do her favorite party thing: stand next to her best friend Cookie, watch the guests in action, and make comments about them, while trying to appear to be talking about something else.

"Now, there's a really good guy. Don't you think?" says Cookie, indicating Jimmy. "Not perfect, I'm sure. If he was, he wouldn't be interesting. And he's getting a little heavy. But strong and hard-working and committed and honest. Just a solid guy. And doesn't he fill the room with sunshine? Even I think he's sexy. And him and Rachel? Boy! What a combo!"

"Yes, to all you just said," says Annie. "It's a shame Rachel is so cool I can't even hate her for being with Jimmy."

Rachel is on the other side of the living room fiercely expressing her opinion about something to a mixed group of partiers. She is a foot and a half shorter than Jimmy, blond to his dark, but with a bigger personality.

Annie sighs.

Cookie changes the subject. "So, what do you think your guy is trying to sell to that bunch over there?"

Denis is holding court with his followers, mostly men and a few women. They stand out from the other partiers by their raucous laughter and rapt attention to Denis's performance. Forbidden cigarette smoke is evident.

Annie says, "I've given up. I don't know what he's doing. I see him and his friends as scumbags and criminals, basically." Annie notices that young Penelope from downstairs is in Denis's crowd and laughing a lot. She's wearing what looks like a cheap "Sexy Pirate" costume from a drugstore, eye patch and three-cornered hat and plastic cutlass and all. Thigh-length boots. She doesn't look bad.

"What do you think about the women in that group?" asks Cookie.

"I don't know what you mean. I barely know them."

"Don't they seem to be dressed a little whorish? Maybe a lot? I'm not judgmental, but you know what I mean."

"Yeah, I guess. It's just a party, Cookie."

Annie goes to get herself another beer. She comes back with three, all opened.

Young Penelope comes over to Annie and Cookie.

Striking an unsteady pose, she says, "What's up, bitches?" too loudly. She pauses, then in a lower voice, "Just kidding. Hi! What's up, sisters?"

Cookie says, "Hey. I'm Carolyn."

Penelope says, "Hi, Carolyn, I'm Penny." Then, to Annie, "I know who you are. Thanks so much for the party!"

"So nice of you to attend."

"You know what I was just thinking?" Penelope asks. "No, of course you don't. I was wondering what color

happiness is." She waits for a reaction from the two
women, and getting none, forges ahead.

"You know how anger is red and jealousy is green, or
maybe envy is, they're kind of the same thing, aren't they?
And cowardice is yellow, but fear isn't the same thing as
cowardice, right? So what color is fear? And what color is
lust?"

"Purple," says Cookie.

Penelope says, "What?"

"Passion is purple."

"But is passion the same thing as lust?" asks Penelope.

"I have no fucking idea," says Cookie.

"But anyway, you get the concept. So, what about
happiness?"

Cookie shrugs.

Penelope soldiers on bravely. "I mean, is it blue, like a
clear blue sky, or like a bluebird? But if you're blue, you're
not happy. You're sad. See what I'm saying?"

Annie finishes her second beer of the three she brought
back "I think happiness is silver and gold."

Penelope considers this. "Hmm. I can kind of get behind
that."

Annie thinks, I just realized that the idiot young woman
standing next to me has been fucking my husband. I know
it. I can feel it. I can smell it. It has a color. I don't know
what color yet. What color is hate?

Annie looks at Cookie swaying to the dance music, who
looks back at her with what she interprets as understanding
and sympathy. But now Cookie and Penelope are dancing
together. They look good. Penelope's sinuous young
sensuality. Cookie's intelligent funky womanhood. They
interact nicely. It's sexy.

Annie chugs her third beer. She decides to leave. She
thinks, I don't belong here.

She doesn't say goodbye to anyone. As she is leaving,
she walks through the kitchen and grabs a pint of bourbon.

Near the door, she passes Pat who is carrying a lit joint to pass around. She snatches the joint and heads out the apartment door.

She stands at the sixth-floor landing and smokes half of Pat's joint, and downs several slugs of bourbon, until she feels like she will soon be thoroughly fucked-up. Then she decides to walk down the stairs. All the way down. Whatever it takes.

This is kind of great. I love these old walkups. There ought to be more of them. Fuck elevators. Except for disabled people. The old walkups are the reason you never saw any fat people in New York back in the day. America is getting soft. But I need to keep track. So, that's one flight.

Annie is on the fifth-floor landing, and notices Penelope's apartment, 5B, which she shares with her boyfriend? husband? named Ray. I wonder what cute little Ray is doing tonight. But no time to think about cute little Ray right now. I need to get down these stairs.

Okay, this is going really well. I'm as sure-footed as a mountain goat. That's number two. This floor is where Charlotte and Beth live, and that's where old Mrs. Rafferty lives, who does the shopping for "the old ladies," Mrs. Piazza and Mrs. Jones, who live on the second floor.

Now we're at number three. I'm really getting into this. I could just keep on going down and down.

Number four. I could do this all day. It feels important. Like a quest. The stairway looks like a steep tunnel going deep into the Earth, to where the ancient mysteries lie.

Number five. Exercise is so good for you!

Number six. Wait a minute. I need to think about this.

Annie has walked down five flights and she is still going down. There was a door at the back of the stairway on the first floor that she never noticed before. She opened it and kept on walking down. Down is all she wants.

It's dark.

She opens the creaky wooden door at the bottom of the stairs and walks onto the dirt floor. The cold damp soil odor almost knocks her over.

She hears a bass voice shouting "Hey, you! Lady! What are you doing down here?" Annie is startled to her core. She sees a big shadowy figure lurching toward her.

Annie feels an icy rush of fear in her chest. She thinks, now I know. Fear is silver. "Well, I live here," she says. Then she gets angry. Anger is blood red after all, she notices.

"What are you doing down here?" she barks back at him. "Who the fuck are you?"

Annie is face-to-face with a large, shirtless, grease-and-soot-covered man. He smells goatish. His muscular torso is streaked with sweat, and something else. Paint? She thanks the fates that she came of age in New York, where aggression can be answered by counter-aggression, and sometimes neutralized by it.

"Have you ever been in the basement of this building before?" he demands. "Did you even know there was one? Have you ever seen that basement door?"

"No."

"That's the way it's supposed to be. You don't belong here."

He continues. "You could be in bad trouble. That would be fun. But not this time. It's a good thing for you that you're supposed to be somewhere else. Up on the fifth floor, talking with somebody up there. Go on, do that, whatever it is. Or don't. I don't care. See what happens. Good night!"

He takes her arm and firmly guides her out of the basement and slams the heavy door that she has never seen before behind her.

Annie ascends the stairs.

Well, okay then, thinks Annie. I guess that's that. Sometimes you just go way too deep.

Annie is finding the trip up the stairs much more arduous than the trip down was. Isn't that always the way? she thinks. What the heck? I do this at least twice a day. The stairway curves in ways she is not expecting.

She arrives at the fifth floor and knocks on the door at 5B. Is this a good idea? she wonders. All the way up she has been rehearsing what she is going to say: Hi, neighbor. I'm wondering if you would like to invite the drunk and stoned lady from upstairs in for a cup of tea. The filthy half-naked guy in the basement says I need to talk with you about something important.

She stashes the half-finished pint of bourbon in the corner next to 5C.

Ray opens the door and says, "Hi! Well, you're the last person I expected to see here. You're throwing a party upstairs, aren't you?"

Cute little Ray is really tall, thinks Annie. She stares up at him and says, "Yeah. I am. Hi, Ray. Just how tall are you?"

"Six foot five. Is everything all right? I'm sorry I couldn't come. I'm getting over a cold and I'm studying for my Boards."

What kind of Boards? Annie wonders. She decides to act normal. "Oh, yes. No worries. Sometimes I need to get away from my own parties. Being an introvert and all. Just thought I'd check in on you." Why? I never have before.

"I know what you mean. I don't do well at parties either. Want to come in?"

"Sure! Thank you! Just for a little bit, though. I've got to get back soon."

The apartment is too warm and has an antique smell of lavender and hot soup.

"Do you want a cup of tea?" asks Ray.

"Thanks, Ray. No, I'd just like to sit down for a little bit."

By the way Ray is acting, Annie figures he knows she is messed up. They have never exchanged more than a few words. Annie sits on the scarlet velvet loveseat. Ray sits on the padded rocking chair across from her and picks up his teacup from the coffee table.

"So," begins Ray, "other than your introvert panic, how's the party going?"

Annie doesn't reply immediately. She looks at Ray for a long, soulful minute, which clearly makes him uncomfortable. She is filled with compassion for him. Yes, he is a sweetie-pie. He's the perfect model of the nice boy. What did the man in the basement want me to talk with him about? And who is that man, anyway? He doesn't know me. He's not the boss of me. Annie chuckles at this last thought.

Annie decides just to get right down to it. "Ray, I want you to know that I am not here to have sex with you." Ray does a great double-take. Annie almost laughs out loud, but then instantly feels insulted. Jeez, I'm only about ten years older than you, twelve at the most, and I know I've still got it. Everybody says so. I'm hotter than your idiot girlfriend. You should be so lucky, chum! The color of the feeling is pink.

The pink feeling subsides, and Annie decides she'd better start over. Maybe that wasn't the best opening. "Ray, what I meant to say is, I think my husband Denis and your Penelope are having an affair. In fact, I'm sure of it. I'm sure even though I don't have any actual proof." She almost says, what do you think about that? And what are you going to do about it? But she doesn't. Let's see what happens, she thinks.

Ray looks stunned. He takes a sip of his tea but doesn't say anything.

Annie is rapidly sobering up. Her heart goes out to poor Ray.

"I'm sorry, Ray," she says.

Ray finally says, "Why would you tell me that? When you don't know for sure? This is very upsetting. You could be wrong."

Annie thinks, but doesn't say, I'm not wrong. I wish I was, honey.

Annie watches Ray's face as he experiences a series of emotions. She wonders what color they are. She thinks she is watching his desire to lash out at her in anger, and then his resolve (sky blue?) to reject that impulse. She feels calm and unafraid.

Annie says, "Ray, I didn't come here to hurt you. I thought you ought to know."

Ray says, "Why? Why should I know? What good does it do me?"

"I figured you'd find out soon enough because neither of them is all that smart, and so they aren't careful. This way you aren't blindsided. You might react impulsively and do something rash. This way you have time to think about what you want to do."

"Did somebody tell you I have a gun? Is that why you're saying that?"

Annie feels another jolt of silver fear. "Do you have a gun, Ray?" she asks.

"No."

"Okay, then! Good!" She is relieved.

"I might get one, though." Ray must have seen the alarm on Annie's face, because he quickly says, "I'm joking, Annie. Bad joke. I'm not the gun type."

Annie doesn't know whether this information is reassuring or not. She is pretty sure Denis has one somewhere, although she's never seen it. And ammo. At least he likes to allude to it. Could be bullshit, though. With him, you never know.

Ray sits still for a long time. Finally, he says, "All right. So, this is what I'm thinking. There are many things a man could do when he gets news like this. Confront his lover.

Confront her lover, if he really is her lover. Tell her to leave. Leave himself. Shoot them both, and probably himself, like they do in the books and songs and news stories. Pretend he doesn't care. Go out and find his own lovers. And so on. All bad options.

"This would be so much simpler if Penelope had told me when it started, if it really did start. But then it would have turned into one of those stupid scenes where I'm angry, she's sorry, she promises it will never happen again, we make up, and then nothing changes, and I'm facing months and months of suspicion, betrayal, and agony. Or she never sees the other man again, but I can never trust her. In either case it's the kiss of death. Once the news has been delivered, whether or not it's true, it's all over for them. Us." Annie believes Ray knows what he's talking about.

"Or you could have decided to keep your mouth shut," Ray says angrily. "Then I wouldn't have to wonder if you're mistaken, or crazy, or have some other motive for telling me. And believe me; I am thinking all those things.

"I have only two choices that don't involve enormous suffering. I can leave her and try to forget her, as fast as possible, or I can wipe tonight out of my memory. I never saw you. This conversation never happened. So that's my choice, Annie. This never happened. So, sorry, you must leave."

Ray stands up and extends his arms to Annie. Annie stands up and accepts the offered hug. He is very warm. She lays her head on his chest and begins to weep softly. He is comforting her, and she doesn't know why. Comforting the woman who might have just wrecked his life.

He says, "This never happened." Annie repeats, "This never happened." She feels better.

He releases her gently and she walks unsteadily toward the door. She turns before she leaves and gives him a little childish wave with her fingers. He waves back at her the same way.

She trudges up the last flight of stairs, opens her door, and walks into her apartment. The party is still going on. Dark Side of the Moon is playing on the stereo.

The crowd has thinned out, creating enough floor space for the games that are happening – a big raucous game of crazy eights and a four-person scrabble game. Denis and Penelope are both in the card game, but they are not sitting next to each other. Most of Denis's crew has left, taking their scumbag vibe with them. Cookie is standing next to the food table, talking with a pretty woman Annie doesn't know. Cookie turns toward Annie when she walks in the door.

"So, there you are, hostess! I was wondering what happened to you! Are you okay? You look a little worse for wear."

Annie replies, "Yup. I just went on a quest."

"Successful?"

"Hard to say. But definitely an experience. I'll tell you about it sometime."

"Hey, while you were questing, you missed all the excitement here!" says Cookie.

"Why? What happened?"

"About half an hour ago this tall guy shows up. Just walks in. Nobody knows him. Really drunk. So, he's lurching around and talking crazy, and he's got his right hand in his coat pocket, and he's saying things like 'where is she?' and "where is that little whore?' and saying he's not going to take it anymore, and he's got something in his pocket for her, implying he's got a gun. And he's knocking stuff over and scaring everybody. A bunch of people just grab their coats and leave. Some of the guys are talking about grabbing him and giving him the bum's rush. Then Denis walks right up to him, and is all friendly and peaceful and simpatico, and gives the guy his whole hey

brother, everything's going to be all right rap. The guy
starts to calm down. Denis is like, 'Come on, pal, your girl
isn't here, let's go out in the hall and talk,' and they do, and
then Denis comes back maybe ten minutes later and says,
'Everything's cool now. He said to tell everybody he's
sorry. I took him downstairs and put him to bed. He's
going to have a monster hangover tomorrow.' I think the
guy was that Penny girl's boyfriend. In the meantime, I put
some mellow music on and got the games started, but half
the crowd had already left."

"Where was Penny all this time?" asks Annie.

"I don't know. I think she was probably hiding in the
bathroom. I didn't see her until after Denis came back."

Cookie says, "Annie, sweetie, you look exhausted. Why
don't you just go to bed? I'm fine. I'll stick around until
everybody leaves and clean up. If anybody asks, I'll tell
them you've got a big day tomorrow. Then I'll call car
service."

Annie looks searchingly into Cookie's face. "Cookie, tell
me the truth. That story you just told me about the guy
from downstairs – you were just playing with me, right?
Because of some of the things I've told you? That didn't
really happen, did it?"

"Annie, I wouldn't do that. Not to you, anyway. It
happened. Ask anybody who was here. Ask Denis."

"Because I was with the guy from downstairs, talking
with him, Penelope's boyfriend, probably about ten
minutes ago. And he was sober."

"It really did happen, Annie. I don't know what to say."

"It couldn't have. Maybe it was a different guy."

Cookie puts her arm around Annie's shoulder and guides
her toward the bedroom. "Okay, Annie, just for tonight
we'll have it your way. It didn't happen. It never happened.
Good night, honey! Don't worry, I'll take care of
everything. Sweet dreams!"

Sister Talk

Elizabeth loved going to her older sister Scarlett's room after supper dishes were washed and homework was done and teeth were brushed and night clothes were put on, to have their nightly talks. They had a ritual. Elizabeth would knock three times on Scarlett's bedroom door. Scarlett would open her door a crack, barely concealing her grin, and say, "Yes, is there something I can do for you, little forest creature?"

"Oh, please let me in. There's a hunter after me!" Elizabeth would reply.

"Well, then, come in and be safe and warm and share my humble home." Scarlett would say, flinging her door open wide.

"This is my favorite time of day!" Elizabeth would say. "What are we going to talk about tonight?"

This evening it was cold and blustery outside, so Elizabeth felt especially safe and warm in Scarlett's room. Scarlett was wearing her cream-colored flannel nightgown with the tiny red and blue flowers, and Elizabeth had on her puppies-and-kittens pajamas. She jumped onto Scarlett's bed and wrapped herself in the big blue comforter. The wind rattled the windows and made that flutelike, whistling noise when it blew across some chink in the house. Elizabeth had just started taking flute lessons at school, so she knew how that sound was made. Mom and Dad called it their little ghost.

Scarlett sat down at her old-fashioned vanity table and began brushing her long auburn hair her nightly one hundred times.

"Tonight, we're going to talk about who and what we are. You do know that we're not really human, right, Elizabeth? You're a smart girl. You must have figured that out by now," Scarlett said matter-of-factly.

"No. I didn't know that. What are we?"

Scarlett pondered. "That's a really good question, dear sister. That's something I've been wondering for years. I haven't decided yet. But I'm getting close. Maybe you can help me figure it out. There are signs."

"What are the signs?"

"Okay. Try this. Can you curl your tongue into a tube, not curled up but curled down? Curled under? Do you know what I mean?"

Elizabeth tried it. "Yes, I know what you mean, and I can do it."

"Now, can you curl your tongue into a double fold? It's hard to explain, so let me show you." Scarlett showed Elizabeth her tongue, folded into a "W" shape. Elizabeth showed Scarlett her own folded tongue.

"Yes! That's it!" Scarlett exclaimed, clapping her hands. "You know, they say you inherit that ability from your mother."

"I think we inherited lots of things from Mom," said Elizabeth. "Do you think she's coming home soon, Scarlett?"

"I don't know, honey. I think so. I sure hope so." They sat and looked at each other for a while.

"Now," Scarlett continued, "Can you wiggle your ears?" Elizabeth proudly demonstrated ear wiggling. "Good," said Scarlett. "Can you wiggle one ear by itself, then the other by itself?" Elizabeth demonstrated again.

"Excellent!" Scarlett said. "Now, how about this? Can you touch the tip of your tongue to the tip of your nose? Very few people can do that."

Both girls did it.

"Wait!" said Elizabeth. "I've got one for you. Can you put your elbow in your ear?" Both girls tried and failed.

"Nobody can do that!" complained Scarlett.

"I saw somebody in my class do it." Elizabeth insisted. "I swear I did. I was right there!"

"Oh, the girls in your class are all little freaks."

"It was a boy," countered Elizabeth. "It was Jimmy."

"Wasn't Jimmy your friend who didn't show up for school one day and never came back?"

"Yes."

"He was a little dickens. Are you sure he didn't just stick his elbow in somebody else's ear?"

Both girls giggled.

"Wait! Wait!" said Elizabeth. "Can you do this with your eyes? Look into my eyes." Elizabeth made her eyeballs vibrate rapidly, an eerie, shimmering effect. Scarlett responded by doing the same thing.

Something large and heavy threw itself against Scarlett's bedroom door repeatedly, making dull thuds. Both girls pretended not to notice.

"Scarlett," Elizabeth asked, "Would you feel my shoulders, please?" The older girl put her fingers on her sister's shoulders. "No, down a little farther. Do you feel those two bumps?" Scarlett did. They felt like the bony ridges at the ends of collar bones. But she thought they were in the wrong place.

"Yes, honey, they're just your bones. You're growing really fast, and you're skinny. Very pretty, but skinny. You'll fill out soon."

"Mom says they're my wings starting to come in."

Scarlett smiled. "Mom likes to make jokes. And she wants you to feel good about yourself. They're just bones."

"Okay."

"So, what's next?" asked Scarlett. "Let's get back to talking about what we really are, since we both agree we're not human."

"Sure," said Elizabeth. "But I've got another one for you. Can you do this?" Elizabeth tilted her head back and shot two jets of red fire out of her nose.

Scarlett leaped up in fright and retreated from Elizabeth until she backed into her closet door with a bang. "Oh my God, Elizabeth! What did you just do?"

"I did this," said Elizabeth. She again expelled two long jets of flame from her nostrils. This time they shot all the way across the room, scorching the lace curtains on the window.

"Wow!" said Scarlett. "I've never seen that! How did you do that?"

"It's like anything else. I just do it."

"You scared me so much, honey. I'm still shaking."

"It's nothing. I won't hurt you, Scarlett, I promise. Want to try it?"

"Sure, I guess so. What should I do? Think about fire?"

"It couldn't hurt."

"Come here and look in my nose," said Scarlett. "Tell me if you see anything. And don't get burned!"

Elizabeth did as she was told. Scarlett repeatedly expelled air out of her nose. Then she stopped, blew her nose on a tissue, and tried it a few more times. Finally, she said, "I've got to stop. I'm getting dizzy. Did I do it? Did you see anything?"

"I saw a few sparks, I think," said Elizabeth. "You're getting the hang of it now. You just need to keep practicing."

The large, heavy object continued to collide with the bedroom door.

"Have you shown anyone else? Mom? Dad? Your friends?"

"Nope," replied Elizabeth.

"Why not?"

"I guess since I've never seen anybody do it, and nobody talks about it, I thought it was one of those things you do when you're by yourself, but you don't tell anybody."

"Is there anything else you can do that you've never told anybody?"

"Well, I can make my hair dance."

"What?"

"I can make my hair dance. See?" Strands of Elizabeth's dark hair lifted themselves up and wove around her head in intricate patterns, coiling into ropes and braids and uncoiling again, looking like beckoning fingers, then flickering flames, then writhing snakes, then graceful dancers, then fields of kelp rippling under the ocean.

Scarlett said, "That was so beautiful, I didn't want it to stop."

The dull impacts on the door continued. Elizabeth said, "We should go and see what it is this time."

Scarlett said, "All right."

Both girls went to the door and opened it cautiously.

"Oh, it's just Chauncey!" Elizabeth exclaimed.

In bounded a very large and smelly Old English Sheepdog, who immediately climbed onto Scarlett's bed.

"Aw, Chauncey sweetie!" Elizabeth jumped onto the bed next to him, put her arms around him, and squeezed tight. "You are the best dog ever. Aren't you, honey? The best, best, best, best dog. And the handsomest! We all love you so much!" Elizabeth kissed the old dog over and over. The sheepdog grinned and panted and licked Elizabeth, and squirmed with delight.

Scarlett rubbed her eyes and shook her head, thinking there was something wrong with her vision. She looked at Chauncey again. There appeared to be parts of him that were transparent, little windows where she could see through his body to whatever was behind him. She kept trying to clear her eyesight, but it didn't work. Elizabeth noticed her sister's dismay.

Scarlett said, "Elizabeth, do you know what's wrong with my eyes?"

Elizabeth said, "I think I do. Are you seeing places on Chauncey where you can look right through him?"

"Yes. Do you know what that means?"

"Chauncey is an old dog. He can't do all the things he used to do. There are parts of him that aren't there anymore. I think you are seeing those parts. I mean not seeing them."

"Did you do this to me? Did you make me see him like this?"

"I didn't do it on purpose."

"Can you see those holes in Chauncey too?"

"Yes."

"As he gets older, will there be more holes?"

"Yes."

"Until he's nothing but holes?"

"Yes."

"Can you make it stop? I mean, for me? Make it so I don't see him that way? I don't like it. I want him to look normal. The way he used to. Seeing him this way makes me too sad."

"I don't know if I can. But I can try." Elizabeth got up from the bed and pulled the dog by his collar. "Come on, Chauncey. Let's go, boy."

"Wait!" Scarlett said. "Do you see anyone else like this?"

"Yes."

"Who?"

"Dad."

"Please make it stop, Elizabeth."

"Okay."

Elizabeth left Scarlett's room with Chauncey and closed the door.

Scarlett sat back down at her vanity table, feeling suddenly tired. She put her head down on her crossed arms. She thought, "Elizabeth, honey, I love you so much. But I don't want what you've got. I want to be like everybody else and not know things." She might have dozed off for a little while. Or maybe not. It was hard to tell.

Scarlett heard three knocks on her bedroom door. She shook herself alert, went to the door, opened it a crack, and said, "Yes, is there something I can do for you, little forest creature?"

There was Elizabeth, with good old Chauncey. They both looked happy and whole.

"Oh, please let me in. There is a hunter after me!"

Scarlett hid her grin.

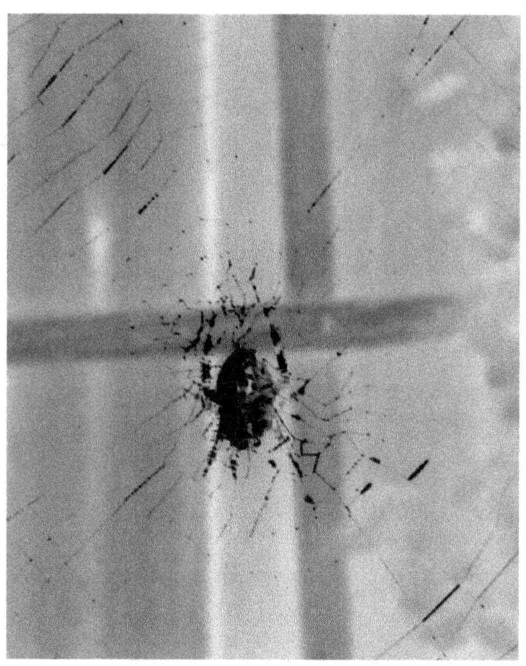

Sara Ries Dziekonski

Sara Ries, a Buffalo native, holds an MFA in poetry from
Chatham University. Her first book, *Come In, We're Open*,
which she wrote about growing up in her parents' diner,
won the Stevens Poetry Manuscript Competition and was
published in June 2010 by the NFSPS Press. Her poem,
"Fish Fry Daughter," was selected by Ted Kooser for
his *American Life in Poetry* column. Ries Dziekonski
taught composition and literature at Erie Community
College before teaching for SENA in Colombia. Her
chapbooks include *Snow Angels on the Living Room
Floor* (Finishing Line Press 2018) and *Marrying
Maracuyá* (Main Street Rag 2021), which won the Cathy
Smith Bowers Chapbook Competition. She lives with her
husband, son, and cat, and works for Keep St. Pete Lit as
an editor and creative writing teacher. She is the co-founder
of Poetry Midwives Editing and Submission Services,
which she offers through Keep St. Pete Lit.

Basket of Peaches

These days, when onesies fill donation bags
faster than wind can tangle hair
as you speed down highways with open windows,

slow things down.
Sit on the soupy sparkling shore
with your husband and ten-month-old,

look at your son's perfect face, teeth:
teeny seashells, then point at the waves rolling in.
Slow things down.

See him squeal and clap.
Sunlit husband, moonrise on our backs,
each wave another chance at elation,

slow things down.
Check in with your good friend in Buffalo
on her daughter's two-month birthday—

*Never before has time been
so obvious,* she says.
Slow things down,

rummage for paper and pen.
Write the poem, even though your basket
of peaches may already be half-eaten.

•Bullet Points

•You blow raspberries
on my legs as I drink strong coffee—
then you use your teeth,
leaving cliff notes on my calves.

•It's one of those days when all
the silverware is dirty. I clean enough
for each meal. You complain
from your high chair—it feels
like waitressing during lunch rush,
and you can change the station completely
with a smile, or silence.

•Strolling with you, my sneaker finds
the only puddle. (We've been rain-
less for weeks.) *What the fuck,* I say
as a lady with floppy hat and poodle
promenade past.

•You don't fall asleep in the stroller
like usual. After zigzagging home
from the park, your blue eyes *still*
open, barely, but enough to slurp
the whole sky.

•The sun is your teddy bear, and
you are my teddy bear sun.

•I walk extra up and down
the shaded lane. A neighbor shouts
from his porch: *You're going to tire
yourself out,* then chuckles, and I think
I'm beyond that. I'm exhausted

to tears.

•You've been on Earth for fifteen
months, so it's fun to pull books off
shelves, make them instruments,
so my favorite poets have crinkled pages
and crooked spines, but I imagine
poem notes adorn your skin
as you tear through pages.

•I write because I am afraid
of the empty drawers of memory,
that these bullet points will become
shells tossed to the floor
once our stomachs are full.

•Bedtime story. I look over
and you're smiling, at me, like you have
some wonderful secret to tell.

Bridges

*published in Cordella Magazine

The contractions
had me writhing
on the ground,
making me
a gateway
to the world.
Palms on the floor
I cried to the nurse:
I don't know what to do.

She straightened
my slipper sock and said
That's what labor is like.

On the monitor we saw
the contractions had gone from hills
to mountains.
Breathe through it
they say
but you wouldn't try to go sailing
mid-hurricane.
Before the contractions
were too steep to climb,

I was dancing through them,
in my olive green hospital gown
joking about my new vintage dress,
belly full from Thai.
The nurse said,
Normally it's jello or popsicles,
that's it.
I was dancing

any which way I felt
my hair dashing this way,
then that,
to the song I put on repeat:
"Bridges"
as I belted out the refrain
I bet you wished you never burned that bridge oh no
'Cause now you'd like to cross it.

Later lying on the crooked bed,
the pain clawing its way through me,
it was clear.
Bodies are bridges,
and there's no other way
of crossing.

How It Ended

You only have to let the soft animal of your body
love what it loves—Mary Oliver

New Year's Eve-Eve, End of 2020:
There's no simple way to say this.
I strolled my baby through the stomach-shattering
stench of my neighbor's dead body
on our way to the back gate—
my parents flung their hands over their mouths.

The rankness ripped through the masks
we wore to keep out COVID,
ransacked our bodies, and for days,
spiders scraped and scratched 'round my intestines—
spun their webs of nau—sea of sickness.

I could not see Dad's expression
through his mask, so I did not know
why he insisted the smell could be
an animal. I'd already told him
It's our neighbor. He died.
We saw the paramedics.
Dad said *But people have animals,*
you know, people sometimes have animals.
I could not see Dad's face
and did not know that he chose
to not understand. So I said,
to make him understand,
Our neighbor's been dead a week!

Then: silence loud
as sirens. I peered
through the window
to his humanness.

It's early 2021, and when I stroll Teddy
around the city, I think of my own animal-self;
the soft animal of my body. My skin, frantic for life,
gulps the air—*please*.

Grandma's Brown Spots

a found poem: from Aunt Cheryl's Facebook comment under a
picture of age-spotted hands with bright pink manicured nails

I remember
my mom always lamented
her brown spots, yet

when she passed,
the only organ
she was able to donate

was her skin.

I was told
the beneficiary
was a burn victim.

Graveyard Shift

published in Blue Collar Review

I return from work, feet throbbing
from having served so many drunks.
I'm in an apartment that I recognize as mine
but the objects feel distant: sound asleep.
The hardwood floors are cold coffin lids.
I light a candle but the wick's too short
so the flame shrinks back to darkness,
and my lover, diluted in dreams,
will not depart from sleep.

I believe the dark mouth of this night
could swallow me, take me off to some foreign place
so I pay attention: Clock says 6:57,
walls gape from fist and nail holes
and the faucet sheds tears on the stainless steel sink.

I'm slightly outside this world,
as I imagine it might feel to be dead,
still part of the whole but somewhat off-center
the way an orange peel must crave
the juice of an orange, and I am worried

that the light will grow outside my window
before I have made it to sleep, so I stop this poem.
I shut the curtains, put on my sleep mask,
yank the covers over my eyes.

The Diner is Up in Flames

and all the customers just sit there,
somber statues in a row
of booths the color of pews,
          and my father was the priest at the grill.
They sit there with folded hands,
waiting
for my father to cook their last meal. I
am floating near the ceiling,
observing it all, the way one does in dreams.
I descend to the grill and scream
                              bloody rare bullets
into my father's face: *Get out of here, hurry—*
But Dad refuses to stop.
He's got orders to cook,
and, they don't call him
Super Dave
for nothing.

lady at the counter

(for women who walk alone at night)

**published in Cathexis Northwest Press*

sisty scuffles into our diner
with her usual bouquet of bags,
orders iced coffee
in the dead of winter.
she unlids a new batch of questions.
today she wants to know
what i think about when i swim,
what my parents are like,
if anything about my childhood
bothers me, if i laughed a lot,
what i found funny.
i grab more ice for her coffee.
she orders a second steak dinner,
says *when i'm upset, i eat,*
her boots crying dirty tears
of snow onto her bags.
i have ice cream most nights, i tell her
to make her feel better.
she presses her palms together,
leans her chin on her fingertips,
says *when my mother died, i ate*
a half-gallon of ice cream,
and for a while, i did that every morning.
i serve her steak, pop a roll in the microwave,
fetch a handful of gold-wrapped butter pats.
she says *i don't drive.*
i like to walk, alone.
i just walk and walk, sometimes all day.
i know, because i see her all the time,
sometimes at three in the morning.

weeks later, as i'm eating my shift meal,
i spot her lumbering down the avenue,
bags bouncing off her thick thighs,
hatless, so her short gray hair
is dusted with snowflakes.
maybe you, like me, think
she's a woman walking alone at night,
she must want company.
i run outside and invite her in.
skin shining with the glow of streetlight,
she smiles and keeps on walking.

George Grace

…with Fine Arts League of Buffalo Best of Show Award winner, *Blast Furnaces under Shrouded Moon* at the Carnegie Cultural Art Center in North Tonawanda, NY, May 2022.

George Grace is the author of three poetry anthologies (two more ready for publication); six plays (all staged); and several short stories. He founded the Circleformance Lit/Music series (1984); and co-founded the LitGarden Writers Group (2008). The second printing of his book, *Steeling America—a Poetic Memoir of Bethlehem Steel's Lackawanna Plant* has been included in the National Steelworkers' Archives in Bethlehem, Pennsylvania.

He has taught workshops for Writers-in-Education, and in Attica and Collins Correctional, and has guest lectured at

Villa Maria College, City Honors High School, and Buffalo State College.

His poetry has found publication in *Earth's Daughters*, *Pure Light Magazine*, the *News Poetry Page* and he took one of the top 8 awards for, "Bagging It" in the Wergle Flomp International Humorous Poetry Contest. He was also on the finalist list (out of some 2700 entries) of Fish Publishing's Short Memoir Poetry Contest, judged by two-time American Poet Laureate, Billy Collins.

He is currently working on a memoir of his twelve Years living in Buffalo's Kenfield Projects, *Project Rats: Growing Up Poor in the Richest Nation* and two poetry anthologies *Wow, Philosophy* and *A Hastening Countdown from Infinity.*

When not writing, George is also a nationally-exhibited and award-winning visual artist, and was past four-term president of the Buffalo Society of Artists. For more information, go to the Buffalo Society of Artists and look him up under the Video Archive Project.

Research Lady

For Donna

Her eyes open with the zeal
of a firefighter's feet, hitting the ground,
running to answer a five-alarmer.

Seconds after *good morning,*
the mattress still warm,
she launches into a narrative from her dream

about *intersectionality* and *micro-aggression.*
She tries to convince me
that the remake of the movie "Ghostbusters"
is *a typical Hollywood metaphor for neoliberal capitalism*
and begins to name names.

Wait, wait, I plead.
Let me open my other eye!
Please!
Let me get a few sips of coffee in me
before you continue!
Make that a big gulp! Or two!

We move to the living room. She chooses the big chair,
props her feet on the bottom shelf of the coffee table,
laptop computer mid-thigh from her upraised knees.

I take my spot on the sofa, adjacent.
Her eyes are masked by the odd sheen-reflection
of the computer screen in her eyeglass lenses,
she taps the keyboard several times, then several times
more.

Looking as if she has become one with the machine,
a lovely cyborg or soulless extraterrestrial,

depending on the tilt of her head,
and the shape of her lips as she speaks,

seeking to answer a question I asked the night before,
she says, *Yes, unfortunately, Walt Whitman was a racist.*

In my best Rocky J. Squirrel falsetto voice, I reply,
Hokey smokes, tell me more, Research-Lady!

The article was long enough, and unimpeachable,
but her impeaching mind looked for more,
chinks in the armor of the article's biography,

yet another hint that nothing is real
until one looks at it from every perspective,
and deep,
deep.

The Lesson of the Hall of Mirrors

When in the shuttered room of your life,
the face in the hall of mirrors becomes too familiar,
cloistered in a concave gossamer reflection,

images more blemished than its bearer's,
yet still recognizable, surrounding you like a catcher's mitt,
grinning or frowning or contorting with you, stopping
when you stop,

or billowing out, a tumescent concave insult to everything
you hoped you'd ever become,

a jarring embarrassment of self-interpretations
remains, festering beneath an impenetrable depth:
that caricature of you that protests the prospect of too little
reward

for trying to view yourself too long, too closely
is not as safely tucked away behind that mirror
as you have deluded yourself to expect,

for trying to better grasp what you've always known best.
Far safer to just turn away when the image gets too large.

Too often, in the absence of a reliable mirror,
the prettiest lies are the ones we tell ourselves.

Ode to the Previously-Published Poem

"The Vice Presidency isn't worth a bucket of warm piss."
(Misquoted to: "...warm spit.")
--John Nance Garner, FDR's Vice President, 1933-41

Dear author--
Read your poetic submission and it strikes us, to be polite,
as
familiar.
As editors, we find it:

More useless than a fire extinguisher in an igloo.
As sensible as center lanes in a parking lot
or automobiles with snorkels.

As readable as the list of nutrients of bottled water.
Less engaging than a flight attendant's instructions for
using seat belts.
As informative as a grave marker where nothing has ever
been buried.

It confines a dried-up idea in an escape-proof prison.
It is Botoxed well past its expiration date.
Lost its poetic virginity and never noticed.
It's like, so-o-o twentieth century.
The train arrived on time to find an empty platform.

The vacant room seven-A,
still stinks of something long dead
after five years
and we don't want to know why.

That's this old poem.

A redundant redundancy.

A clichéd cliché.
More worn than flip-flops on a sandpaper treadmill.
The vice-president of poems.
It has seen better days
with editors that didn't know better.

Time to move on,
to go where so few third-rate poets have gone before:

Irrevocably discouraged.

Fishing with My Brother

*"We didn't think it would end this way for him. We thought
one of us would kill him."*

      --My brother's best friend, at his memorial

I once dreamt of a hazy morning on a mirrored lake,
on a dock, in a boat, didn't matter which,
nowhere else to be, no one waiting for us,
lines in the water, and you said,

Three hours out here.
I think the fish have gone on vacation.

But that didn't matter, either.
I was with my big brother,
and you told me about women,
warned me away from drugs
helped me prep for my SATs.

I have dreamt of you, showing me how to frame a house
mud fresh drywall, pitch and hit a fastball,
keep a marriage together with humor
when you're not certain how you'll make the rent,

dreamt of you, picking up your daughter
squeezing her so hard and saying
this is how to love your children:
be there, always, and hug them,
even when they think they hate you.

I have dreamt of sitting by your bedside in your final hours
holding your hand, afraid to let you go,
saying *thank you for teaching me how to be a man,*

knowing there can never be another you.

But these dreams are the fire lit windows of every cozy
home in Thomas Kincaid's hamlets,
fictions bleached of moments with pulses,
Utopias and Shangri-Las scrubbed of harsh reminders
that too often people you want to love
just don't care,
and there's no sense wasting time wondering why.

Now having run out of time,
you find yourself holding a severed fishing line,
using your last breaths
to blame your sour fortune on the water,
the fish,
and the fishing partner.

The Hidden Cost of Memory

Like cadavers rising unbidden
from the graveyards of my past,
they call me in muted twilight voices,
impatient for me to discover dark artifacts
more deeply buried in their glitzy, spangled piles.

In process of taking inventory
of this mausoleum above my shoulders,
I find myself avoiding altogether
those memories with jagged razor edges,
handling gingerly the brittle ones
hidden in their shadowed depths.

Separating treasures from trash,
I move some to the forefront
of my memory's showroom,
knowing that even joyous recollections
may bring sorrow
when reaching for those which might never have been.

Lunar Lament

I wasn't the one who landed on the moon.
Not second, third, or fourth.
Didn't qualify.

I didn't hop around
in four-billion-year-old virgin moon-and-asteroid dust
with Collins watching from orbit, wondering
Why couldn't that have been me?

Like Collins in the command module,
I could only watch as my planet
orbited Armstrong and Aldrin on the moon.

For their time there, they were the center of the universe.

Sure, had the landing or rendezvous failed,
Collins would have come home alone,
and likely suffered a survivor's guilt,
leaving him no other recourse than to
not survive,
either.

Perhaps after a warm breakfast
and a warmer shower.

I didn't walk on the moon.
Accident of birth,
(Too young; not fit enough; wrong city;
parents who could never imagine me in a space suit)

dictated I wander amidst millions of ordinary
Earthbound people

seeking my immortality writing poetry,
painting artworks,
no rescue mission summoned or even necessary.

Sometimes, I imagine myself brooding,
stranded,
standing in moon dust,
wanting more than anything a cool glass of water,
some clean air to sweeten my lungs,
and the good wishes of some dear friends
to reel me back to the love of a warm home
under an envelope of blue.

Becoming a Poet Forced Me

to think with words.

For the first third of my life,
I couldn't, and didn't have to, journey very far from home
to find flora and fauna I could not name.

I was okay with robins. They hopped
around on my lawn, pulling up meals
of *filet le ver* (*Worms*. Yum).

And sparrows, irritating in moochy numbers
ever nervous, close to my feet,
hoping for bread crumbs spilled from my table.

And daffodils, roses. Tulips, too--each testing
what little I knew about seasonal appearances.
Cherries had a season. Pears, apples, blueberries, too.

Season ends. Tough luck. You have to wait another year.

As I never saw or heard of a mango until it was too late
to mention it in a high school essay, this condemned me,
I'm sure, to a community college education

where I got beyond grade- and high school grunting
and urban project berserkerisms,
and delved into more arcane nouns and verbs.

Limited by poverty to wherever I could walk or bike,
it was dogs, cats, squirrels,
horses and cattle seen only in Westerns,

mean trees I fell out of, but couldn't name.

And now, as I finish reading this poem
and ready myself to leave this thingamajig
with the doohickey, attached to the frammas unit,
I ask the crucial question:

How was I to know that to become a real poet,
I'd have to learn to name things?

Checkout Line

I felt his eyes on me as I rolled my cart,
filled with foodstuffs, up to the counter.
I knew what he was thinking: *It never fails,*

around the fifteenth of every month.
Welfare recipients. Sponging off the taxpayers.
Paying for all that with food stamps.

He unloaded his cart.
Fifteen Abrams tanks. Four F-35 fighter jets.
A five-thousand-dollar toilet seat. Connecting bolts,
one thousand dollars apiece.
Mountains of Filet Mignon-priced Meals Ready to Eat.
Thirty drones.
A brand-new aircraft carrier.

Just as it looked as if he was about to say something to me
I launched a preemptive strike.
Excuse me, sir, I said.
I saw you here last month, buying a nuclear sub.

Yes, he replied. *I like nuclear subs.*

I didn't know you could buy those things with food stamps.

I don't use food stamps. I pay with cash,
unlike some people, he sneered,
ignoring my broccoli and salmon to glare at my Cheez-Its.

The cashier pretended not to be listening
as she scanned each of his items, the prices flashing
eight-and nine-digit numbers on the cash register screen.

Damn it, he said, rifling through his credit cards.
I forgot my shoppers' bonus card.
Any chance I could use yours?

I sighed. *Yeah, what the hell. Here.*

You think he might have thanked me for helping him save
three hundred and forty-seven million dollars
and change
on this shopping excursion,
but he mumbled, *leech*
as he strained to push his cart out the door.

Plastic Tigers

Look, the optimist says.
With flora and fauna displaced by asphalt and condos

erased by overfishing, global climate change,
and toxic spills,
clear cutting, agricultural runoff, and poaching
yes, we're losing thirty or forty species a year to extinction.

But there's an up-side to this:
Remember the little plastic dinosaurs you bought
at the science museum when you were a boy?
Because we have plastic
we can now make newly-extinct species immortal, in a way.

By entering them into a database
with 3-d printing,
we could produce commemorative models
in real time   as they pass

tie yellow ribbons around their little plastic legs
to inject a sentimental dimension to our losses
and make a killing
excuse the pun
selling them in toy stores and zoos.

Kids love this stuff.

Check this out, he says, opening his briefcase.
I've gotten ahead of the curve.

He holds up a molded & painted Bengal tiger
minus the fur, claws, heart, eyes,
the menacing growl,

and the sense of doom
one feels when facing the real thing.

They could go any day now,
and when they do,
I'll be ready.
I've got a manufacturer in China
pumping out 20 thousand of these an hour.

See?
Grief is marketable.

Joe Todaro

Joe Todaro was born and raised in the North Park area, and migrated in the early 90s to the West Side Elmwood environs during a time of Sunday Rose Garden drum circles, clinic defense, Circular Word Books, Topic Cafe, 3B's, Cybeles and the original Pink Flamingo; hatching conspiracies over nocturnal omelettes, drying out at Towne Restaurant, and breakfasting at Preservation Hall. Of alternative currency, involved in Network of Light, Good River, Urban Epiphany, Classics on Elmwood recitals and a legendary Diamond Tribe song sojourn now known as Cheaper Than Vinyl. Joe's big return in 2002 from the California Bay Area followed four years of existential ruse; then as now and here in current form.

America Revisited (2021)

America, it was all too much and then I looked again.
America, the math doesn't add up, it never did.
The stairs get more tedious by the year and I get more lazy.
America I can make this my magnum opus
        if I stay up late enough and sustain my attention.
I have jaundiced fingers, fevered neuroses,
        food remnants on my keyboard.

America now is my moment and I wish it weren't.
I come from Five Points Bowery, from Little Caesar's gate
Prince and Mulberry,
        brownstone shadow burning carbon across my face.
America your refrigerators rolled out as soon as the Great
War ended,
        televisions everywhere after the next one.
        Korea gave us Elvis, Vietnam - the moon landing.
We conquered and purchased the rest since then.
        I'm still waiting for the prize.

America I made the long Pyrrhic climb to the top floor
        but found it empty.
This mythology of yours is getting winded.
I get it mixed up reciting to others.
        You can smell the suspicion at the cafe.
America I weep during MacArthur's West Point speech
        and collect Grateful Dead memorabilia.

I am young Benchley, I am Savio,
I am the Thanatopsis Club
        Midtown, brandy-slinging literati of a gilded age.
I am the golden spike of Sacramento.
I have the might of a Carnegie steel mill.
I am Old Man Astor fur-trapping in the Ozarks,

scores of peddlers back in east-side coonskin dens,
plucking pianos in cubicles across town.

America if it's your self-image, I have a pill for that too.
How else can I put this?
America, the Titans have departed one way or another.
We may well be all we have left.

Indolence, an Ode

This means moments, hours-long
when one can rest upon chair of choice
and consider the wind outdoors;
nothing like a house that's silent
but for its own breath,
in late winter forced-air shimmer,
tinnitus like cicadas under fridge murmur;

There will be a slow hum of cars,
of doors and stair-steps;
a vast negotiation beyond that door.
Here is a steaming cup of coffee,
water bottle over the evening's pills,
some sheet music, a pen;
I remember a fervor in acquiring these things
but now they are here.

They show us images of un-realness
many forms; follow us
into our tender sinews of understanding;
foretell, depict, re-tell, repeat.
So it is well to acknowledge the real -
Left hand, creased, holds down
the opposite page;
here, upon summon of these eyes.

1970s Kitchenette

I don't miss that vile haddock
with the damn lemon,
took me two decades to realize
there is other seafood.
The salad: iceberg with
oil and vinegar in an afterthought
clump next to four or five string beans.

This amid ICU lighting,
brown and tan tiles, green linoleum,
fake-pine laminated cabinets,
fridge and table like Buicks
built to withstand a Soviet squall.

I brought some dinner
over to the folks the other day,
pulled some sushi from a paper bag.
They looked confused.

He / She / They

I said "they" but it didn't fly.
Must've lost the way between him and her,
and *they* wasn't keen.
So much for lunch.

"Is you is or is you ain't what he said 'they' is?"

What *they* said was almost as confusing when I said it to
her,
and him,
but it was *they* who stole the occasion.

Later, I saw *them* across the street and waved, to no avail.
The he and she of it all was all *they* was trying to get
across,
though language and history proved too fierce.

She felt like "they," but the genetics didn't agree,
leaving them and *them* bereft.

(She or) *they* can argue with *their* own chromosomes,
but I'll still wave from the curb
on my end.

Vigils

Don't get yr sleekits in a bunch
ye Carmelite nymphs with your petrichor aura,
ye scrim and scree 'til wee hours of marn' ,
I admit screeing along ever-darn even' .

Am I too touched for you, too rampant in me pate?
Tongue too sharp for yr starry dark confessions?
I'll give ye reason fr real
amid my earth-hewn new moon cairns, these

jagg'd twigs of alchemy these thousand years,
even yr medieval pyres can't burn 'em all.

Images (2003)

Now take a look at this one,
mid-1940s
she was about 21
had been overseas
nurse duty.
Came back changed,
they said.

She helped out at the bar
carried people home
busted some jaws too
she took no bull, this one,
used to go dirt biking
through the hills outside of town.

That stare,
the certainty of that chin,
clearness of her gaze,
agate necklace she got in Morocco.

Call these up next time you visit her -
she might seem sweet and helpless -
she's a badass.

And what will become of the likes of us?

asked the cashier with her eyes,
as I bagged the bread and eggs.

Is this the ageless tale they breathless told
around council fires, hunched over quickening coals,
faces cracked from salt and sand?

Something perhaps of a response in swiping my card,
I lacked all words in the decorum
of a weekday evening,

managing nods of thanks
as ourselves as passing orbs, she,

briefly at ease, until turning her eyes
to my successor to ask anew.

Gaslight Deity

Old Frostbeard set down
his vast goblet, and upon belch and wipe
of chin said,
Let there be light
apparently,
and may have been kidding,

what we ended up with,
constant as a Buffalo spring,
or the feeble strobe from my pixelate screen,
was a light too indifferent for corners,
nuances, or nooks.

No, it was an indolent god
dispensing pearls among the pleasant,
glory for the comfortable,
leaving the rest to cobble
replicas from scrap metal,
fallen rivets,
halogen and anguish.

The Great Resignation

Having spent the last few rounds
of entreaties
the ballot boxes
petitions
marches
thundered oratory

songs
poems
grisly photography
nefarious still-life artistry
ribbons
tiny pennants and flags half mast

all impotent
meaningless
you can guess
what's next
when they realize

there's nothing
for them
to extract
from others

it's theirs to
take.

Brevity

This rises from a white sea,
as a song from stillness
coaxed into being.

Know it by name or thread or sounding
thing resting here. Find it here,
then fade to white.

Scott W. Williams

Born 1943 on Staten Island, NY: Raised in Baltimore, BS (Mathematics and Humanities) at Morgan State University in 1964; PhD in Mathematics (Topology) at Lehigh University in 1969.
Worked at IBM (product testing), Penn State (post-doc), Institute for Medicine and Math (Ford Foundation Fellow), Charles University in Prague (Fulbright Professor), Beijing Teacher's University (adjunct Professor). Research Professor at the University of Buffalo 1971-2013.
Since 2013 published: 14 poems published, 1 poetry chapbook, 1 poetry & micro fiction chapbook, 3 poetry & flash fiction anthologies.

Train Man

Published in Juniper Poetry 2017

Decades before the eight-lane expressway,
years before one could hike,
its ten miles splitting Baltimore city.
Daddy and I stand high over the Jones Falls Valley
Looking south from the North Avenue Bridge.

Pennsylvania Railroad on the east side.
A smaller B&O Railroad on the west side.
Jones Falls River among the trees in between.
Both train stations are in sight.

Six lanes of cars, trucks, buses, and trolleys
at our backs, rumbling under our feet,
Fumes in the air, dust and grime on our skin
None dissuaded the joy of watching trains with him.

Son, what's coming on track 1,
what's coming on track 2?
And it was good to sing a train man's song:
All aboard on 1, express train to Chicago,
arriving on 2, the Limited from New York.

And it was good, standing close
Kent cigarettes and later Camel breath
soft kind face, small mustache, sad eyes.
Tan wrinkled very strong hands.

And stopped in the station, a soft engine idle feels organic.
The thrill as electric powered engines
WHINnnE underneath.

The wind-whisper of smooth fast Pennsylvania express
trains, their dopplered sound anticlimactic as they move
north and south.

The sure CHUNKACHUMK, CHUNKACHUMK is sweet
with the deep heavy B&O diesel freight **GROWL**
Pulling endless freight trains hammering and shrieking
Allegheny coal all the way from West Virginia.

No steam engines, no **chooga** chooga chooga.
Still the flavor, the variance, the odor of trains
While standing on the North Avenue bridge
Couldn't be trucked, traded, or transformed.

Son, what's coming on track 1,
what's coming on track 2?
Dad, it's all aboard, the Harrisburg Express
to the African Methodist Episcopal Zion
Colored Peoples' cemetery.

hot dog delights

Published in Le Mot Juste 2018

I was glad when my mother's day was filled with Music
or meetings 'cause I smelled *hot dog* water.
Eating out with Dad or him cooking at home, *hot dogs,*
skinless or with the well-done natural casing crunchy skin-
on texture; *hot dogs* with mustard, or ketchup and/or relish
from the Pennsylvania Dutch; *hot dogs* with plain white
rolls or sour dough rolls or whole grain rolls; *hot dogs* with
sauerkraut with or without mayonnaise or sautéed peppers
and onions; *hot dogs* with ground beef   and a side of onion
rings.

In college, we expanded. It was reverence, eating *hot dogs*
cooked in beer, ale or stout, or with chili powder. A late
night meal of *hot dogs* smothered in bacon or bacon bits or
topped with fava beans, pinto beans, tomato vinaigrette,
mashed potato, canned corn and jalapeño salsa. Yes, it was
like **Kama-dog-sutra**, the **Kamasutra** of *hot dogs*, trying
food positions, we enjoyed it every way without or with
Swiss or Muenster or Camembert or Cheese Whiz. And our
taste for *hot dogs* expanded to wursts, Knockwurst and
Knackwurst and Bratwurst.

Dad is gone and I grill my *hot dog*s blackened. In stores
now, *hot dogs* are all beef, or mixed pork and beef, all veal
or mixed pork and veal. Popular with my kids is Pizza
stuffed in *hot dogs* or *hot dogs* on pizza. In suburbia
discover the new "Fish dogs," *hot dogs* topped with

calamari, clams, lobster, mussels or salmon and a butter
sauce. My new wife demands Turkey dogs or veggie dogs.
In the end, the overwhelming extras give witness to all our
slurping, grinding, popping, sucking, and suckling sauces
delightfully dribbling down our throats disguising our hot
dogs.

At The Forge

Published in Juniper Poetry 2019

Waamp! Waamp! Waamp!
bing bing!
Waamp! Waamp! Waamp!
Bing! da bing!

I love the rhythm and sound.
Hammer on steel & anvil.
I love the flexing of muscles
in arm, shoulders, and back.
Attention minus thinking as I hammer.

Waamp! Waamp! Waamp!
Bing da bing!

Search and remove fire impurities.
Metal filings and stones steal heat.
Shovel more coal and grow heat.
Make a white hot cave of coal.
To put the rod in the cave.

Waamp! Waamp! Waamp!
Bing da bing!

The rod's black shifts, reddening comes.
Sun-white sparking starting to burn steel.
Ungloved hand holding other end of steel.
Lift steel from cave to the big anvil.
The striking hammer hand relaxed.
Mind is silent, observant

Time to forge metal onto itself.
Welding steel, **Waamp! Waamp!**

Hit anvil rhythm, *bing!*
To weld steel Waamp! Waamp! Waamp!
Anvil rhythm goes *bing da bing!*

Hit steel, Waamp! Waamp!

Forged until molecules attached.
The two places are now one.
Mind remains silent, observant
Prepared to change metal's shape.
Prepared to change my attitude.

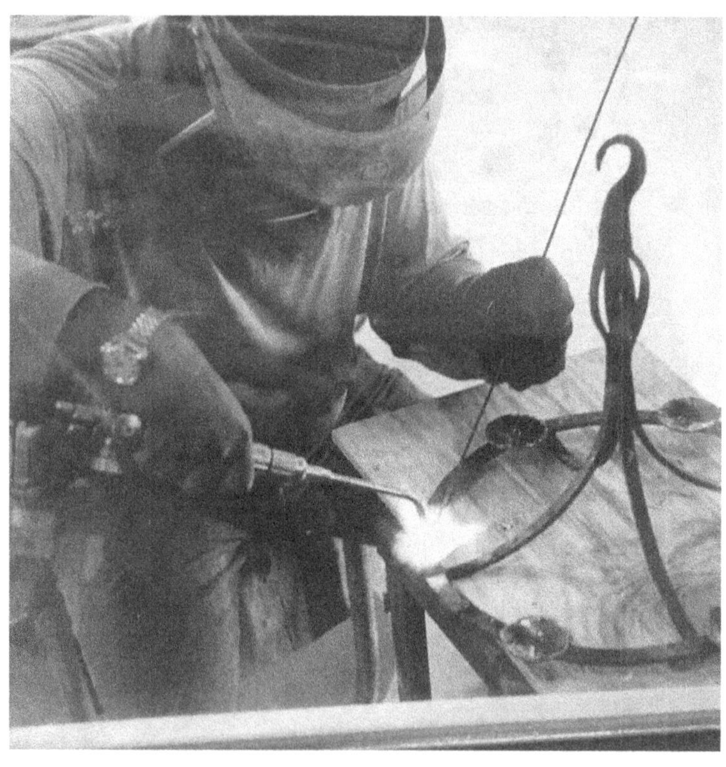

Eight Leos

For Rachael Keri Williams 2021

Published in Oddball Magazine

When my first daughter
was born July 27,
my father planted a tree
and said, "Study Pope Leo VIII."

A planet-struck astrologer wrote,
"Rachael has eight Leos in her chart
like Leo VIII, Antipope for a year."

I understood the pine tree
standing now at 45 years -
not the eight Leos
nor the Pope from a no-church father.

Leo VIII was Antipope 963 to 964.
and good Pope 964 to till 969 death.
A Cancer with eight Leos in his chart.

I wondered were there wilted trees that made
Leo VIII Antipope or just politics?
Will my girl be Black anti-daughter,
and then good daughter,
when the evergreen tree dies?

John XII made the papal treasury his wallet,
though he opened a brothel he and cardinals frequented,
and he was killed by a husband he cuckolded.
John XII was Pope, never antipope.

Nor was there an antipope like Boniface VIII
who practiced threesomes with
        two men,
        a cardinal and wife,
        a mother and daughter.

Did Leo VIII
        practice bestiality like Benedict IX?
        make his street urchin lover a cardinal like Julius III?
        hold open air orgies like Alexander VI?
Was his body riddled with syphilis scars like Julius II?

Did an antipope die in bed with
        a pageboy like Paul II?
        his nephew lover like Sixtus IV?
        his son's wife like Leo X?
        his mistress' daughter like Sergius III?

If Leo VIII is the sole antipope,
and then a good Pope.
What was the transformation?
Why did my father mention him?
What does eight Leos mean anyway?

Those damn roaring
eight Leos
run my family.

BEFORE THE ELECTION

Published in Mason Street Review 2021

You heard them white mens sayin',
Leave, don't vote or we shoot.

Ol' car motor keep stallin'.
We gotta follow dat north star,
awhile.

Kappy Kaepernick's barkin'
will lead dem crackers to us.
Chain him to the backyard fence.
He better there than house pissin' and shittin'.
We gonna be back soon as 'lection stuff is over.

Kappy will watch the place while we gone.
He a dog. They can be outside all year.
Leave him two bowls of kibble
in his shed.
Fill that bin
by the tree with water.

I got some ripe apples and unripe pears.
Bag a coupla days of clothes.
We gonna just wait out this thing
with folk in the city.

Blown over, we come back
an' everything be alright.

Seven Senryu for Emmett Till

published by Punch Drunk Press 2018

i. - 1955

Mother sends son south
fourteen learning from old folks
Safe with grandparents.

ii.

Did Emmett whistle?
Did he forget he was a
Nigger in Dixie?

iii.

Did Emmett Till flirt?
White woman said he flirted.
How did the boy die?

iv.

Two cut out his eyes.
Two beat and shot and drowned him.
Two said, "Justice done!"

v.

Two White men accused.
Two admitted killing him.
Two were acquitted.

vi.

South returns her son
Disfigured beyond belief
Mom shows his body.

vii-2017, 62 years later

White men are now dead.
White woman breaks her silence
She tells us, "I lied."

Kings Garden

Versions published in Scryptic Mag 2017

Once there was a king whose daughter was beautiful.
He loved her very deeply and he wished to have more.

So he cut her into pieces, and each was an astonishing
    daughter.
Still he wished more and he cut those pieces into pieces,
    and again each was a stunning girl.

He loved these so, that he cut the pieces of the pieces into
    pieces and he loved each of the pieces of the pieces of
    the pieces so he induced.

When he was all done, with love he threw all the scattered
    remains into the air so very high that when they fell to
    earth, rainbowed flowers bloomed and cantered at his
    feet.

Kate Willoughby

Kate wrote her first poem at age seven about a bird alighting on her hand. Her mother gave up smoking in order to afford piano lessons for her, and taught her how to grow tomatoes. Kate grew up playing hard scrabble baseball with the boys, hugging trees, and wanting just three things – a typewriter, the complete works of Shakespeare, and to be just like Nancy Drew.

She wields an editor's sword and shield with the LitGarden Writers' workshop, and her poems and stories appear in *The Buffalo News*, Gary Earl Ross' *Nickel City Nights,* and the speculative fiction anthologies, *A Flash of Dark, Volumes 2* and *3*. Her poem, "Truth" was published in Slipstream magazine, Summer 2022 issue. With her friend and fellow writer, George Grace, she co-edited the first LitGarden poetry anthology, *Just Twelve More Poems*, and co-edited this LitGarden Anthology II, *Tilting Toward the Moon.*

Since retiring from her career as a Buffalo teacher, Kate has more time to dance, rehab her 129- year-old house on the West Side, and build community green spaces with Grassroots Gardens. She still loves birds, baseball, and trees.

One Blue Heron

Someone has to keep an eye on things,
says Billy Collins, custodian of cirrus clouds,
who would notice the coldness of this bottle of beer,
whose words I take as dharma, the path of truth;
breathe in light; let it out, now, now, now.

Sitting on a bench at Reinstein Pond,
I mark the inner stillness of this one blue heron on a log,
who, like me, seems to wait for early frogs,
who are most likely still asleep for winter.

Deciding it is time to go, I fold my newspaper,
swig the last drops of my beer.

The heron cries, *Enough,*
and rises up.

Gratitude

The Haudenosaunee praise the gifts
of Earth, Father Sky, four winds, stars, waters.
Tibetan monks begin their day
with songs of equanimity in joy and suffering.

I wake up late and curse the pewter skies,
crack the mirror with my crabby face,
slick back my cow-licked hair, rub crusty eyes,
and fester over faults of yesterday.

But rain, soft as gray doves' wings,
shines up the black onyx city streets,
releases sweetness as it damps
the dying leaves all dancing in the yard.

And in my little kitchen is a man
who makes my morning coffee, toast with jam.
I take the mug in my unworthy hands.
I look at him and say, *Thanks, thanks.*

Morning

bees buzz   hot and yellow frequencies jazz through
me
a song in my head radio   broadcasts from the lyric
universe
        that metaphysical jukebox
        surfing the waves
the   leaping peaks   the sloping valleys

hey! Spotify or 97 Rock's got nothin'…

this morning Mustang *Sally*
rides bareback out of bed   puts on stretchy splashy skin
        shapes-shifts me into super-me
        something   someone
else   who's not an old schoolteacher
        frowning at clocks   using up red pens

She's My Cherry Pie slam-chases me up the stairs
        to where dawn gold-washes the rafters
            all the high clear spaces
and the maple ballet barre scolds my cold knees to relevé!
        Up, Up on toes!
                            I make
strong   long   allongé arabesques break
        over the floor in waves and waves
flowing into spiraling ochos   Metallica's tango
        Nothing Else Matters
slower now

as Bach's *Partitas* turn the volume down
I come to rest in lotus pose, open my antennae, and let in
        serenading clouds of gas and dust
        the crystal songs of stars and galaxies.

Paradise at the Polish Cadets'

Seventeen steps led to Heaven with a scuffed dance floor,
and I ran up all of them, my heart
already thumping in a boogie-woogie beat,
and man, did I look good in my tangerine twin set
folded down ankle socks, little clean white Keds
bouffant pony-tail, lipstick by Maybelline!

I didn't have to wait long, tapping feet
to *Rhythm Sundae* with The Earl Hines Band
before tall Patrick caught my eye, grabbed my hand,
spun me out in a double-tuck Lindy-turn.

The earth sure moved for me,
but it was just the floor -
with Benny's clarinet jumpin' as we all let out a roar -
Rrrrring! Pennsylvania six-five thousand!

Young Jim cut in on *Sing Sing Sing,*
slippery with sweat, triple twirling
me, breathless, hot,
hearing the angels swing.

Nesting

> *Even the sparrow finds a home, and the swallow a nest for herself...*   - Psalm 84:3

With dirty cabinet-washing water running down my arms,
I take this moment to breathe, arch, and straighten,
look out the kitchen window at my muddy April garden
where a common Old World Sparrow
gathers dried-up ferns and grasses, chooses bits of twigs,
flits with her mouthful up to the neighbor's eaves
to build her new expectant nest.

Not so alone now, I scrub off grease, and time.
This has helped –
this taking out of everything to look at it -
rusted cans, rancid oils, cracked cups -
discarding expirations, broken bowls,
reaching far into the corner cupboards
for griefs I thought I'd thrown away.

Then, everything cleaned,
I place back only what is useful -
like the sparrow,
making room for something yet to come.

-Previously published in the May 15, 2022 Sunday edition
of *The Buffalo News*, page F3

Goodness

Staunch yellow jacket,
I watch you grasp in your forelegs
a chunk of the lunchmeat turkey
you bit off from the bigger piece
I have set aside for you on the porch railing
so that you do not go for the sandwich on my plate.

You rise up, lumbering under its weight,
to feed the larvae or your queen awaiting in the nest,
which I hope, loyal warrior, is nowhere nearby.

At your successful take-off, we say *Huzzah!*
and having nothing else to do this quiet September noon,
we wait for your expected return.

Devout, patient, doggedly civic-minded,
you deserve all the goodness
you can find in this universe,
all that can be given you -

just like the rest of us
who forage in the wild.

Hydra

Invincible flowering dogwood,
your tangled profusion of cross-webbed,
red-stemmed branches
now invades adjacent lilacs,
smothers struggling oak hydrangeas.

Like Hercules,
tasked to tame the many-headed Hydra,
undaunted by its immortality,
I take up handsaw, pruners, shears,
rough tools to hack and clip the thicket
of snapping dead and living limbs.

When I can beat nothing else,
when lightning ignites the open places,
the invisible wind brings death,
and we have to be alone,
I think of Hercules
dipping his arrows in the virulent Hydra blood,
taking a cure from the venom,
preparing to fight again.

Eight Degrees

I heft the Target bags out of my rusty Subaru,
and stand dumbstruck in the dark ice-rutted street
transfixed by clustered stars, in the February sky,
that frost, sharp as a new knife, has cut to diamond clarity.

The Seven Sisters of The Pleiades -
bright daughters of Atlas and Pleione:
Asterope, Merope, Electra, Maia,
Celaeno, Taygeta, and young Alcyone
evade Orion's wrath in blue-hot female unity.

In the west, small Ceres pauses in her astral loop,
looks in on them as mothers do,
to moderate the rules of law, of birth and death,
nodding to the Full Wolf Moon -
the hard tree-crackling "Frost-Exploding Moon" -
ensuring that we all are in our place.

In love with cold and fractal light,
not ready to go home,
I take a bit of cracker from my bag
to crumble on the ground
in tribute to strong sisters,
in thanks for mothers who check in,
to nights of scintillating quiet,
and the great illuminated mystery,
that, in this moment, never really ends.

Blood

Pitching a pick-up game in the middle of May, all the guys
were there, and they loved it that I could really throw some
meatballs right over the plate so they could all get some
action and a chance at a base hit,
because, let's face it, it's all about democracy.

Back then, I could hit some dingers too,
right up over the school roof -
I only did that with my own cheap balls,
not to waste some other kids money,
so mostly I hit some line drives and grounders right down
the alley to give them some practice with their fielding.

Some dude always got smacked in the face on a bounce,
or their glasses knocked off on a short hop,
and there was plenty of blood coming out of noses.
Nobody went home to clean up.
And we weren't afraid to lose a little skin sliding into base
either, even though we played on the macadam of the
school parking lot, the bags, only chalked boxes,
home base, at best, a flattened cereal box.

So this one May day it was pretty hot,
and I had changed after school into these cute blue-and-
white checked shorts and a white camp shirt, made two
braids, bangs stuck to my forehead with sweat.
I was just 13, but had already been kissed on the lips
by Bobby Helwig against the chain link fence behind the
playground, and I had my own mitt.
We were all there that day, doing our best to act tough and
have fun, me, being the only girl, also acting as umpire.

After breaking up a shoving match over the legality of
stealing home, I realized I had to pee, and feeling a sudden
dampness in my shorts, began to jog home, thinking I was
about to wet my pants, which would be the ultimate
embarrassment in front of all those boys.
I made it home, banged up the stairs,
slamming the bathroom door behind me.

You can probably guess that it was blood, and a lot of it,
but Mom had given me the talk,
and I didn't pass out
or think I was dying.
But the supplies were, for some unknown reason,
out in the hallway cupboard.
I soaked my ruined shorts and underwear in cold water,
washed myself, then just sat on the toilet for a while,
wondering if the guys were still out there,
and what if they had seen the blood.
Did they know about girls,
and were they completely grossed out?
I didn't know if I could face them again.

Mom would be home from work soon.
She had had a hysterectomy when I was five,
so she didn't need the girl things - the napkins - herself,
but made sure I had some on board.
Then I had an awful thought –
what if my Dad had to use the one and only bathroom?
He could just come up at any time, and there I'd be,
stranded, with no pants.

I wrapped a bath towel around my middle,
and cautiously opened the door.
The coast was clear, so I got the supplies, pads, sanitary
belt, and raced back to the bathroom to put it on.

Then, towel-wrapped and clean, I went to my bedroom and lay down, rubbed my aching stomach, and tuned my transistor radio to WKBW.
The Temptations began to sing:

> *Sunshine, blue skies, please go away*
> *My girl has found another and gone away*
> *With her went my future, my life is filled with gloom*
> *So, day after day, I stayed locked up in my room*
> *I know to you it might sound strange*
> *But I wish it would rain, oh, yeah, yeah, yeah, yeah*
> *(How I wish that it would rain)**

*The Temptations - *Wish It Would Rain* is a studio album by the Temptations, released in 1968 via Gordy Records. It was the final release from the group's "Classic-5" era, during which David Ruffin, Eddie Kendricks, Paul Williams, Melvin Franklin, and Otis Williams constituted the Temptations' lineup. *Wish it Would Rain* was written by Rodger Penzabene, Barrett Strong, and Norman Whitfield.

Just One Thing

I get up. I walk, I fall down.
Meanwhile, I keep dancing.
                    – Daniel Hillel

Somewhere, there is just one thing -
a true book, a full cup, a hickory wand,
a sword you could pull out of a high bright stone -
one thing that could fix everything -

if only you said the right word,
or were fond of drama,
and could bang thunder together,
calling up a clean, ravaging wind
to paint in the sky a picture
of a less strange and frightening time.

We can all find ourselves in our place -

    even if it is small,
    it can still have a garden.

Until then, I will get up,
wanting,
walk a little ways,
take a punch, and fall down,
still looking for that one thing,
and laughing,
get up again.

Kintsugi

> *"There is a crack in everything, that's how the light gets in."*   - Leonard Cohen

Spread out the old newspaper,
assemble waxed paper, pottery glue, powdered gold, brush,
to fix this little cracked blue earthenware pitcher
some craft-art connoisseur
gave me for my first-time wedding.

Some things will never be repaired, and shouldn't be.

But this little dent-lipped pot isn't one of those things.
This, I want to keep, to remind me about beauty
and brokenness -
that not everything about the marriage was bad,
even when it left me shattered in some places,
scuffed up, chipped,
but still good for something,

good for many things.

Mix the gilded paste, smooth the sharp edges,
bring together the empty spaces,
burnish the surface with love and precision.

Then, let it rest.

It can hold cream again, or maybe small flowers.

Roof

I try
I really try
to carry on well
as can be expected:
roasting a lemon chicken
stripping off the dirty bedsheets
planting marigold seeds in little pots
blasting Led Zeppelin, Bon Jovi, and Styx
at the very threshold of ear bleeding volume
just to drown-out distract from the never-ending
pulsing whine of the gas-powered cast iron compressor
drone of incessant sharp pop-slapping of the pneumatic
air- nailer, the shove rip and shoosh of four layers of
disintegrating asphalt sliding on its scrabbly slope
from peak to the edge where it crashes without
apology onto my insufficiently- tarped Rose of
Sharon burying completely the tender-shooted
variegated hostas low- creeping jenny and
maidenhair fern yet to emerge. It was just
like the noise in my head sick-banging
like an endless MRI when you ran out
on me, shattering the straight framed
walls I built with blood and nail by
nail by board. I carry on holding
up the rafters, bracing the ridge
overhead, laying new courses,
catching the rain guttering
down in my own
two hands.

Reading *Orwell's Roses* *

We have short memories, and convenient -
like a new mother in joy at her nursing child
puts away the pain, the blood, and afterbirth -
for if remembered, she might never have another.

What comfort we derive, ignoring history,
bricking up the chronicles of suffering
like outlawed books on some forgotten shelf:
child labor in the mines of Pennsylvania,
the Great Smog of 1952 in London killing thousands,
the "terror famine" of the starving in Ukraine.

Instead we focus on the next bright shiny toy,
a celebrity breakup, an actress' skin routine.

And so we go from day to night to day,
forgetting all the tigers chasing us,
and all the tigers we outran before,
never learning how to keep away from them,
dangling from the cliff again,
admiring the one red strawberry as we fall.

Orwell's Roses, Rebecca Solnit, New York: Viking
(2021)